PLYMOUTH DISTRICT LIBRARY

**Removed from
library collection**

D1384957

MAR 1 9 2005

APR 2 9 2005

Plymouth District Library
223 S Main Street
Plymouth, MI 48170-1687

636.7
S

7/00
DW

ILLUSTRATED ENCYCLOPEDIA

DOG BREEDS
OF THE WORLD

MIKE STOCKMAN MRCVS

PHOTOGRAPHY BY JOHN DANIELS

LORENZ BOOKS

Plymouth District Library
223 S Main Street
Plymouth, MI 48170-1687

This edition published by Lorenz Books

Lorenz Books is an imprint of
Anness Publishing Limited
Hermes House, 88-89 Blackfriars Road, London SE1 8HA

© Anness Publishing Limited 1998, 1999

Published in the USA by Lorenz Books
Anness Publishing Inc., 27 West 20th Street, New York, NY 10011;
(800) 354-9657

This edition distributed in Canada by Raincoast Books
8680 Cambie Street, Vancouver, British Columbia V6P 6M9

All rights reserved. No part of this publication may be reproduced,
stored in a retrieval system, or transmitted in any way or by any means,
electronic, mechanical, photocopying, recording or otherwise, without
the prior written permission of the copyright holder.

A CIP catalogue record for this book is available from the British Library

ISBN 0-7548-0021-0

Publisher: Joanna Lorenz
Project Editor: Fiona Eaton
Editorial Assistant: Emma Gray
Designer: Michael Morey
Cover Design: Balley Design Associates
Photographer: John Daniels
Additional photography pp158-160 by Jane Burton

Previously published as *The New Guide to Dog Breeds* and, as part of a larger compendium,
The Complete Dog Book

Printed and bound in Hong Kong

1 3 5 7 9 10 8 6 4 2

Contents

Introducing the Pedigree Dog   4

The Hound Group   6

The Gundog (Sporting) Group   32

The Terrier Group   56

The Utility (Non-sporting) Group   78

The Working Group   98

The Toy Group   140

Index   158

Acknowledgements   160

INTRODUCING THE PEDIGREE DOG

The enormous number of different pedigree dogs recognized today are all derived from a creature that first associated with human beings many thousands of years ago. When humans found out how to light fires, the precursor of the dog must have been keen to share their warmth, and to also scavenge for left-over food. Humans soon realized that the dogs could be put to good use as assistant hunters,

Europe, but the records of such movements are not clear. What can be stated at best is that most of the breeds that form pedigree dogdom in Britain, Europe and the USA today are of relatively recent origin – 200-550 years old. Some of them can only be traced back to the nineteenth century.

A pedigree is the written record of a dog's genealogy for at least three generations.

HOUNDS

As the name suggests, these are the hunting dogs. The so-called sight-hounds (Greyhound, Afghan Hound, Borzoi, Irish Wolfhound, Saluki, Whippet, Deerhound) do their chasing by direct sight, whereas the scent-hounds (Beagles, Bloodhounds, Bassets) use their noses on the ground to follow their target. The Finnish Spitz is unusual in that its purpose is

The barkless Basenji.

The German Wire-haired Pointer.

The Lakeland Terrier.

guards and companions. They would also soon have realized that some dogs were better at one job than another, so for breeding they selected the best for each task, and this, in a nutshell, describes everything that has happened since.

The classic prick-eared hunting hound seen for hundreds of years in the Mediterranean area, from Egypt and Malta to Ibiza and Tenerife, is still with us, virtually unchanged, in two breeds, the Ibizan Hound and the Pharaoh Hound. Most breeds trace their ancestry by much vaguer routes. The mastiffs of the world, for instance, possibly originated in Tibet and, over the centuries, moved with traders and seafarers through Asia and

A purebred is a dog whose parents belong to the same breed and who share unmixed descent since the recognition of the breed.

THE GROUPS

Dogs are divided into six groups in Britain – Hounds, Gundogs, Terriers, Utility, Working and Toy. In the United States and some other countries dogs are divided into seven groups – Sporting, Hounds, Working, Terriers, Toy, Non-Sporting and Herding. Allocating breeds to a group is not always easy, and there are variations between kennel clubs in different countries. Such variations to the groupings used here are noted in brackets.

to find birds, specifically the capercaillie, and to indicate to the hunter the bird's presence up a tree by standing by it and barking.

As a general characteristic, hounds tend to concentrate on the chase and not to listen to the entreaties of their owners to come back to base. They do not regularly figure in the placings in advanced obedience tests. They also have loud voices, which they are not averse to using.

GUNDOGS (SPORTING)

These dogs assist in finding and catching feathered and furry game. The group includes the setters and pointers, which indicate where birds are; the retrievers, which fetch shot birds, hare and rabbits; spaniels, which do both jobs; and a large number of breeds, most of them from the European mainland, which are collectively known as the Hunt, Point and Retrieve (HPR) breeds.

Gundogs tend to be kindly, gentle creatures, tractable and not noisy. They are not all suited to living in towns rather than rural areas, but they are capable of adapting to family life.

might be the "Companion Group". In the Utility group you will find the Bulldog, the Dalmatian, the Poodles, the Japanese Akita (Working), the Schnauzer, the Chow Chow and the Shih Tzu (Toy).

As a generalization, the term "companion" does indeed cover them all, but there are varying degrees of companionability, and these are discussed under the individual breeds.

TOYS

This is a group of small dogs, but they are not to be regarded as ladies' pets. The group includes such characters as the Chihuahuas, the King Charles Spaniel, the Yorkshire Terrier and the Japanese Chin. They are normally kept as pets, but they are clever and can be trained to perform in obedience tests; the Papillon is a good example. They are brave, as shown by the Pug and the

The French Bulldog.

The German Shepherd Dog.

The Belgian Griffon.

TERRIERS

This crowd are the rodent-operators of the canine world. They vary in size from the Airedale, the tallest, down through the Fox Terrier and the Lakeland Terrier, medium, to the West Highland White and Norwich Terrier, the shorter-legged varieties.

They are generally smart dogs, sharp in appearance and character; they are all vocal to a degree; and they make excellent pets as they adapt extremely well to castle or cottage.

UTILITY (NON-SPORTING)

This cosmopolitan bunch seems to include all the breeds that did not fit comfortably into any of the other groups. A more acceptable name

WORKING (WORKING, HERDING)

Working covers a multitude of breeds. There are guard dogs such as Boxers, Rottweilers and Bullmastiffs; herding breeds, such as Border Collies and Shetland Sheepdogs, which in the US form the Herding Group; and all-purpose breeds such as the German Shepherd Dog. Sizes range from the Great Dane to the Pembroke Corgi.

Temperament and trainability vary tremendously; the ranks of the Working Group include many breeds that make excellent household pets and obedience competitors. As a group it has expanded enormously in terms of the number of breeds since the middle of the twentieth century.

Pekingese; and they make wonderful companions, the Cavalier King Charles Spaniel being a favourite.

These groups include almost two hundred different breeds. The pedigree dog has its critics who tell us that mongrels are more intelligent, tractable and healthy, and that they outshine the purebred canines, but the great advantage of the pedigree animal is that it is much more predictable. If you mate two Golden Retrievers you will get Golden Retriever puppies.

In the following descriptions the height is always measured at the withers (shoulders). Heights and weights are given either as a range or an average.

The Hound Group

The temperament of any breed should be as important to prospective owners as size or appearance, although it is one factor that cannot be exactly described or standardized. Official Kennel Club breed standards do contain clauses under the heading "Temperament", but these describe the ideal. Included here are observed traits that may not always conform to the ideal.

What is accepted by most dog-minded folk is that hounds are basically hunters and have been bred to work over all kinds of terrain searching out different quarries. To take on any hound as a companion or family animal and expect it not to behave as a hunter is misguided. Some hound breeds can more readily be taught new tricks than others but it is never easy.

Some breeds in the Hound Group, such as the Beagle and the Whippet, are extremely popular, while others are virtually unknown and unobtainable outside their country of origin.

♦ FACING PAGE **Deerhound**

AFGHAN HOUND

◆ LEFT
The Afghan is an ancient breed. It was discovered by the western world in the nineteenth century.

The Afghan, one of the most glamorous breeds, has a superbly elegant silky coat on an athletic frame, as befits a hunting creature originating in the mountains of Afghanistan.

The Afghan's expression is one of dignity and superiority, but he can have moments of hectic eccentricity, racing across garden or field.

Not inclined to heed the wishes of an exasperated owner unless handled with firmness as he grows up, this is a dog that is not for the uncommitted. Treating one casually will not lead to a happy relationship in the household.

More than capable of acting as a watchdog, the Afghan may use his powerful teeth on intruders if his warnings are not heeded.

In spite of standing over 70 cm (27½ in) at the withers, he is not a greedy feeder; in fact he may be a little finicky if allowed to have his own way. He is an athlete and needs a lot of exercise to cope with his restless energy.

BREED BOX

Size	medium-large
	dog: 70–74 cm
	(27½–29 in), 27 kg
	(60 lb)
	bitch: 63–69 cm
	(25–27 in), 22.5 kg
	(50 lb)
Grooming	frequent and
	thorough
Exercise	essential
Feeding	medium
Temperament	wary of strangers

The Afghan's silky coat will not look its best without constant care. It needs regular and thorough grooming, and any knots must be removed every day. The breeder from whom he is purchased will show the new owner how this is best done.

The Afghan is a dog for the true enthusiast who has the time and the patience to get the best out of a canine glamour star.

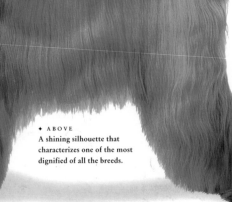

◆ ABOVE
A shining silhouette that characterizes one of the most dignified of all the breeds.

◆ ABOVE
The Afghan's eyes look straight through you, one of the truly glamorous expressions of dogdom; they seem to defy you to resist them.

BASENJI

The Basenji may originally have come from the Middle East, but is regarded as of Central African (Congo) derivation from some three hundred years ago. Certainly that is the area from which the breed was exported in the mid 1930s.

A neat dog of sharp outlines with stiffly upright ears, he has a square-frame standing around 43 cm (17 in) high, and ending with a tightly curled tail. He attracts a small but enthusiastic following with his gentle, friendly attitude. He has a questioning

+ LEFT
Sharp outlines on a neat dog, the Basenji is renowned for his cleanliness and for being odour-free.

BREED BOX

Size	small-medium dog: 43 cm (17 in), 11 kg (24 lb) bitch: 40 cm (16 in), 9.5 kg (21 lb)
Grooming	minimal
Exercise	reasonable
Feeding	undemanding
Temperament	intelligent, affectionate

look on his wedge-shaped face and a wrinkled brow; his curiosity is a real feature of his temperament.

He is known for the unusual fact that he does not give voice by way of a bark but has a yodel-type cry.

The Basenji's short, close-fitting coat is sleek and very easy to groom; he comes in variations of black and white, and red and white, with an occasional tricolour, and he has a tendency to carry out his own grooming in the manner of a cat.

The Basenji's movement is clipped in style and suggests that he is quite tireless, although he does not require an excessive amount of exercise. He will not cost much to feed. All in all, he is a dog that will suit most households because he is thoroughly companionable.

+ LEFT
Poised to spring even from a lying position, the Basenji gives the impression of constant restlessness. He will hunt any form of vermin.

+ ABOVE
The Basenji is always alert, with a permanent frowning, quizzical expression.

BASSET FAUVE DE BRETAGNE

♦ LEFT
It is the ability to adopt such a relaxed pose, while keeping the eyes "on target", that makes all the Basset-types look so loveable.

All the Bassets originated in France. They vary greatly in size, colour, shape and coat type. The Fauve is one of the shortest, standing around 35 cm (14 in) at the withers, but he is neater and has a more terrier-like appearance than his cousins.

Almost always a reddish fawn colour, he possesses a harsh and tough-textured coat. Strangely enough, he does need a bath more often than one might expect, because he is an expert at picking up the odd odour of the countryside!

The Fauve is a true hunter with a surprising turn of speed, especially if his sights are fixed on a retreating rabbit; like so many hounds, once into the chase, he may not heed his owner's call to return to base in a hurry.

A dog that really enjoys life and people, his small size makes him a natural for the growing family; he can be picked up by children. He is not a greedy dog but at the same time he is not choosy about the contents of his food-bowl.

BREED BOX

Size	small
	32–38 cm (12½–15 in), 16–18 kg (35–39½lb)
Grooming	relatively easy
Exercise	moderate
Feeding	undemanding
Temperament	busy and cheerful

♦ RIGHT
A harsh, tight coat on the Fauve makes him easy to groom wherever he hunts.

GRAND BASSET GRIFFON VENDEEN

The Grand Basset Griffon Vendeen is another of the Basset family, and even in his native France is not numerous, which is a pity as he is a kindly, intelligent dog.

He stands up to 45 cm (18 in) at the withers on his tiptoes, and he is not a hefty hound. He is nimble and purposeful in his style of going and gives the impression of enjoying life to the full as long as he is given things to do. He will put his mind to all sorts of exercise that appeal to his sense of fun.

Like most of his type he enjoys his food, but he does not seem to object to being rationed to keep him trimly athletic. He has a rough coat that is basically white with lemon, orange, tricolour or grizzle markings; underneath the top-coat he sports a thick undercoat, so he is fairly weatherproof and easy to keep clean.

A breed that deserves

popularity as long as it is not inbred any more than is inevitable with a small pool of breeding stock.

♦ BELOW
The GBGV has a merry disposition and takes to any sort of canine activity with enthusiasm.

BREED BOX

Size	small-medium maximum 45 cm (18 in), 18–20 kg (39½–44 lb)
Grooming	relatively easy
Exercise	essential
Feeding	undemanding
Temperament	friendly and humorous

BASSET HOUND

◆ BELOW
The Basset Hound is a cheerful character
even if his expression could be described as
lugubrious.

The Basset Hound is the best known of the Basset group, originating in France. His normal prey is the hare, which he follows in a persistent, lumbering fashion. He can break into a run, but his natural pace is steady over long distances.

In spite of the fact that he stands about 38 cm (15 in) at the withers, he weighs around 32 kg (70 lb), which makes him a big dog on short legs. If he has to be lifted into the car or on to

BREED BOX

Size	low-slung but heavy dog: 33–38 cm (13–15 in), 22.5 kg (50 lb) bitch: 33 cm (13 in), 19.5 kg (43 lb)
Grooming	relatively easy
Exercise	steady but necessary
Feeding	has a hearty appetite
Temperament	placid but loud

the veterinary consulting-room table, he may present a problem to the slightly built owner.

He has a reasonably hearty appetite, which may lead him to put on an inordinate amount of weight, especially as he can be idle given the opportunity. As befits a hunting hound with a big chest, his voice is akin to the sound of a ship's foghorn. This can come as a distinct surprise to those in the immediate vicinity, but it

should never give the impression that he is of an unfriendly disposition.

At first sight the Basset looks as if his skin was made for more dog than it contains, and there are a certain amount of wrinkles on his forehead. His most exaggerated feature is the length of his ears; this has been allowed to increase to the extent that he can tread on his ears with ease. As a result the flaps can be injured and their weight can cause problems by interfering with the circulation of air into the ear canal. The droop of his lower eyelids can also cause problems.

The Basset's forelegs tend to twist outwards below the wrist, and this may produce limb problems. His short smooth coat is easy to keep clean and wholesome even if he does rather enjoy rolling in various offensive-smelling farmyard and country substances.

The Basset Hound is for the enthusiast who wants to take on a canine companion of great character as a member of the family.

◆ RIGHT
The Basset Hound usually comes in black, white and tan, or in lemon and white. His coat is easily kept clean and tidy.

PETIT BASSET GRIFFON VENDEEN

The Petit Basset Griffon Vendeen, or PBGV as he is known to his multitude of admirers, has rapidly increased in popularity over the last 25 years, since he began to be exported from his native France. All French hounds are expected to be able to do their job, and this fellow is no exception. He is a bustler of a dog, seemingly never able to sit still. Hence he is for the active and tolerant only.

◆ LEFT AND BELOW LEFT
Cheeky-faced PBGVs positively swarmed across the Channel between their native France and the UK in the mid-1970s, and it was not long before they migrated on to the United States.

BREED BOX

Size	small
	dog: 34–38 cm
	(13½–15 in), 19 kg
	(42 lb)
	bitch: 35.5 cm (14 in),
	18 kg (39½ lb)
Grooming	necessary
Exercise	essential
Feeding	reasonable
Temperament	happy and extroverted

The PBGV stands up to 38 cm (15 in) at the withers; his length is greater than his height, but not to an exaggerated degree – in other words, he does not suffer from problems with his intervertebral discs to any extent.

On his sturdy, well-proportioned body he sports a rough, harsh top-coat with a thick undercoat, which together make him weatherproof. He is inclined to get muddy on his country rambles. He has lengthy eyebrows, so a curry comb is a good grooming tool. He needs good feeding to supply the energy that exudes from him at all times.

The PBGV is not a dog for a town-dwelling family that never visits the countryside.

◆ RIGHT
The Petit Basset Griffon Vendeen is a rough-and-ready breed, built to face all weather and ground conditions.

BEAGLE

As a breed, Beagles produce their puppies easily in reasonable numbers and seem to accept a life in kennels in philosophical fashion. As a result they have been bred extensively for use in medical/veterinary research laboratories, making them victims of their own super-friendly temperaments.

From the point of view of life as a member of a human household, they are similarly accommodating. They enjoy being part of a gang in much the same way as they make good team-members of a pack hunting hares. They are tidy creatures, although they are not always easy to housetrain. Their short waterproof coat makes them drip-dry in the foulest of weathers. Even after a day running across clay, a quick sponge-down soon makes them acceptable in the kitchen.

The Beagle is not greedy, though life in hunt kennels tends to make him swallow his daily ration fast. He is not prone to veterinary problems and lives to a reasonably ripe old age.

It is unusual to see a Beagle winning an obedience competition, as the breed has a tendency not to stay around for the recall once off the lead.

This is a breed that pleases families who lead active lives.

✦ LEFT
Beagles are hunters with handsome muzzles designed to make a thorough job of sniffing out their quarry.

BREED BOX	
Size	small 33–40 cm (13–16 in), 9 kg (20 lb)
Grooming	easy
Exercise	considerable
Feeding	reasonable
Temperament	genially stubborn

✦ RIGHT
Tough forelegs and tight feet make the Beagle able to last all day whatever the activity, in the field, the park or the garden, as long as there's human company.

BLOODHOUND

The Bloodhound is a big dog with a mind of his own. As he stands some 66 cm (26 in) at the withers and can weigh up to 55 kg (121 lb), he is heavy. He is also clumsy, with a tendency to pursue his path regardless of obstacles such as ditches, walls and fences. Once on collar and lead, he may choose to take his handler on without great regard to physical or vocal opposition.

Most people will be familiar with the breed's appearance; the Bloodhound

◆ ABOVE
The Bloodhound has a history as the number-one tracker of the canine world. His long ears are said to sweep scent from the trail up into his large nostrils.

◆ RIGHT
His deep chest gives him good lung capacity.

BREED BOX

Size	massive dog: 63–69 cm (25–27 in), 41 kg (90 lb) bitch: 58–63 cm (23–25 in), 36 kg (79 lb)
Grooming	easy but extensive
Exercise	ponderous but considerable
Feeding	demanding
Temperament	requires understanding

has a super-abundant quantity of skin overhanging his eyes, and this is often accompanied by sagging lower eyelids. His ears hang low on his skull in pendulous folds, and these are said to sweep scents from the ground into his large nostrils and over his highly efficient olfactory mechanism.

His large body is supported by massive bones, but the bloodhound has suffered over the generations from

hip-joints that cannot always take the strain of conveying him along head-down on the scent.

Bloodhounds eat massively and greedily. As with other breeds that have deep chests and wide bellies, the Bloodhound suffers from more than his fair share of a condition called bloat in which the gases in the stomach tend to be produced in great quantities. For various anatomical reasons these cannot be belched in the normal fashion and may lead to torsion of the stomach, which is rapidly fatal unless veterinary intervention is prompt.

The general advice is to feed small quantities several times a day and not to take a Bloodhound out for exercise on a full stomach. It is wise to ask a breeder offering puppies for sale about the incidence of bloat in the ancestry of sire and dam.

Bloodhounds, like most giant breeds, tend not to live to a ripe old age.

Most Bloodhounds are dignified and affectionate, but this is not a breed with which to take liberties as they can take exception to undue familiarity. Properly handled by those who are prepared to understand them, they are a fascinating breed to live with.

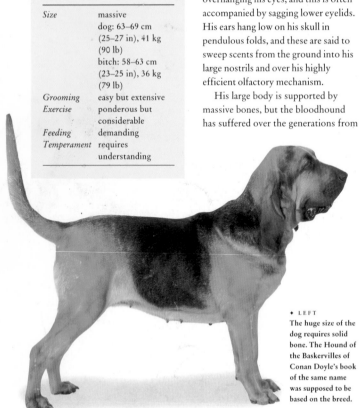

◆ LEFT
The huge size of the dog requires solid bone. The Hound of the Baskervilles of Conan Doyle's book of the same name was supposed to be based on the breed.

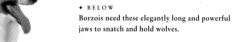

BORZOI

♦ BELOW
Borzois need these elegantly long and powerful jaws to snatch and hold wolves.

The Borzoi, as befits a hound from Russia that was dedicated to hunting wolves, is tall, aristocratic in bearing, and possesses a pair of impressive jaws. His height at the withers is a minimum of 74 cm (29 in), which makes him tall by anyone's standards.

BREED BOX

Size	tall and elegant dog: 74 cm (29 in), 41 kg (90 lb) bitch: 68 cm (27 in), 34 kg (75 lb)
Grooming	regular and thorough
Exercise	moderate
Feeding	not excessive
Temperament	requires understanding

♦ ABOVE
A gentle expression in the eyes belies the fact that the breed can have a slightly fierce temperament.

Added to his height is a lean head, shaped to give an impression of supercilious aristocracy, carried on an arched, longish neck that runs into well laid-back shoulders; all of which produces a superlative representative of the sight-hound group.

The silky coat varies in length over different areas of the body; it requires enthusiastic handling from an owner willing to learn from an expert.

These dogs are capable of running at tremendous speed but do not demand great amounts of exercise. A Borzoi does not have a large appetite, and is not particularly choosy. He is usually faithful to his owner and reasonably biddable.

The Borzoi gives the impression of being fond of people but it is wise not to take liberties with such a creature; he is capable, on occasion, of becoming dangerous if he is annoyed. Such behaviour is rare, but there is some suspicion that certain strains inherit a less than perfect temperament. It would be as well to look into this further before deciding to take on a Borzoi.

♦ RIGHT
The immensely variable pattern of coat colours is one of the distinctive features of this noble Russian breed.

DACHSHUNDS

The Dachshund breed comes in six
varieties. They vary in weight from
under 5 kg (11 lb) in the case of the
miniatures, to 9-12 kg (20-26½ lb) in
the case of the standards. They also
vary in coat-type being divided into
Long-haired, Smooth-haired and
Wire-haired versions.

◆ RIGHT
The Standard
Smooth-haired – if
any of the six
varieties of
Dachshund is to be
considered the
original, this is it.
The body lines are
neat and trim.

◆ LEFT
The depth of the
chest between the
front legs of this
Standard Smooth-
haired is very
obvious.

◆ BELOW
The name Dachshund translates literally as
badger dog and as such reveals its original use
in following badgers to ground.

All six varieties are similar in body-
shape, being low to the ground in
order to be able to go to ground after
their prey, which is generally
considered to be the badger (although

◆ BELOW
The Standard
Long-haired is
the glamour
dog of the
sextet – same
lines masked by
silky hair.

BREED BOX

Size	small–medium
	Standard: 9–12 kg
	(20–26½ lb)
	Miniature:
	maximum 4.5 kg
	(10 lb)
Grooming	varies with variety
Exercise	reasonable
Feeding	undemanding
Temperament	independent

they will do an equally good job if
required to go after a fox).

In the past all the varieties suffered
from severe problems with their backs,
basically because there was a tendency
to breed for longer backs without due
consideration being given to the
musculature needed to cope with that
structural build. Today there is a much
better overall type, but it is wise to
seek out breeders who can
demonstrate a sound strain. Grooming
of Smooth-haired and Wire-haired

◆ RIGHT
All versions should have
a bold head carriage and
an intelligent expression.

♦ RIGHT AND FAR RIGHT
The head of all the varieties of
Dachshund tapers uniformly to the
tip of the nose.

varieties is straight-forward, but the
Long-haired has a soft, straight coat
that does need regular attention.

Exercise is accepted readily by all
six varieties, but they are not over-
demanding on the matter. From the
feeding viewpoint they are all also
undemanding good eaters.

Temperamentally they are sharp as
far as acting as sentinels around the
family premises and possessions is
concerned, and they will not hesitate to
use their teeth if pushed. They are loud
barkers, and the smaller sizes have a
tendency to yap, but they stop once the
intruder has been pointed out. They
make excellent companion animals and
deservedly attract a large following.

♦ BELOW
The Wire-haired coat was developed to protect
these hunting dogs from thorn bushes and briar.

♦ ABOVE
The Miniature
Dachshunds may
have been used to
follow smaller
animals to ground,
such as the rabbit,
the stoat and the
hare.

♦ RIGHT
The Miniature Wire-
haired has a harsh
coat and a small
moustache.

♦ ABOVE LEFT
Breeding between
the different coat
types was banned
very early on in
Germany.

♦ ABOVE
The Dachshund is an
affectionate and
companionable dog.

DEERHOUND

✦ RIGHT
The Deerhound has been used to hunt
red deer for a thousand years.

The Deerhound (Scottish Deerhound) hails from Scotland and is in fact a Greyhound with a harsh and shaggy overcoat. It is said that he has hunted deer for a thousand years, and ancient depictions of him suggest that he has altered little over the centuries. He appears to capture the heart of all who fall under his spell, but in return he demands great loyalty.

He stands 76 cm (30 in) and weighs around 45 kg (100 lb), so he is not a lightweight, but he has a surprising ability to curl up in a corner and not get in the way, even in a small house. He is not a big eater and gives the impression that ordinary oatmeal would be welcome along with the venison.

Grooming should be regular but is not a chore as the harshness of his shaggy coat renders him relatively easy to keep tidy.

As far as his temperament is concerned he is a friendly, faithful creature with a dignified attitude to strangers. One of the most venerated among his breeders travels with a team of Deerhounds from the outer regions of mid-west Scotland to shows all over Britain and does so by train, which must say something about the breed's charm and adaptability.

BREED BOX	
Size	medium–large dog: 76 cm (30 in), 45.5 kg (100 lb) bitch: 71 cm (28 in), 36.5 kg (80½ lb)
Grooming	moderate
Exercise	moderate
Feeding	medium
Temperament	highly companionable

✦ ABOVE
The shaggy coat comes in mainly
pastel shades, from grey through
brindle to fawn.

✦ ABOVE
A narrowish front shows the depth of
chest displayed by all sight hounds.

ELKHOUND

The Elkhound (Norwegian Elkhound) hails from Norway where he hunts the elk, known as the moose in the US. The hound has to be solidly built to take on such a large form of quarry. The attitude of the Norwegians to this native breed is that he should be nimble, quick and courageous whether he is destined for the hunt or is to become a household companion. He fulfils these dual expectations.

◆ LEFT
Elkhounds are solid, and their legs and feet must be powerful to carry them.

BREED BOX

Size	medium
	dog: 52 cm (20½ in), 23 kg (50 lb)
	bitch: 49 cm (19 in), 20 kg (44 lb)
Grooming	reasonably easy
Exercise	moderate
Feeding	has a reasonably hearty appetite
Temperament	highly companionable

◆ BELOW AND FAR LEFT
As well as being powerfully built to cope with hunting elks, Elkhounds need the intelligence demonstrated by these bright, sensitive eyes and sharp ears.

Within the group, the spitz types have pricked ears and tails that curl up over their backs. The Elkhound is a true spitz; he has another characteristic of the type – a loud voice, which he enjoys using. He is basically friendly, but intruders could be forgiven for doubting it.

The Elkhound's coat, which is basically grey, makes him weatherproof. It is a delight to clean by sponging off the worst mud, letting it dry and then brushing it vigorously.

He stands around 52 cm (20½ in) at the withers, and his body is solidly chunky at 23 kg (50 lb). To keep his powerful shape he eats well and may need careful rationing. Elkhounds tend to live to a ripe old age and are a good choice for the active family.

FINNISH SPITZ

◆ BELOW
The Finnish Spitz's outline is as
sharp as his hearing.

The Finnish Spitz (Non-sporting
Group) is the national dog of Finland,
and the Finns are very fussy about his
appearance, which is very striking. He
is bright red in colour and in early
puppyhood looks like a fox cub.
When he grows up he has stiffly
pricked ears and a tail that curls up
over his back. His coat is easy to
clean off and brush up.

He grows to a maximum of 50 cm
(20 in) but weighs at best a mere 16 kg
(35 lb). He is a pocket-sized athlete,
the nearest thing to perpetual motion,
and he loves to be part of a pack. He is
used in Finland to search out the
whereabouts of birds, most
particularly the capercaillie (a large
grouse), and is the only member of the
Hound Group whose objective is a
bird. His reaction to a successful hunt
is to tell the world in a strident voice,
which he also uses at home.

The Finnish Spitz is not greedy; he
lives a reasonably long life, giving joy
to his friends; and he expects to be

part of the household. In other words
he is a healthy extrovert and considers
that those who own him should be
similarly healthy and extrovert.
Whether the neighbours would agree
is a point to be considered.

BREED BOX	
Size	small-medium dog: 43–50 cm (17–20 in) bitch: 39–45 cm (15–18 in), 14–16 kg (31–35 lb)
Grooming	easy
Exercise	moderate
Feeding	undemanding
Temperament	noisy, needs understanding

◆ LEFT
He has a loud voice which he uses often – this is
a very characteristic pose.

◆ ABOVE
That appealing look will change quickly if
you relax.

FOXHOUND

♦ LEFT
Foxhounds are much bigger in the flesh than when viewed in a painted hunt scene. They are not ideally suited to be companion animals.

The Foxhound (English Foxhound) rarely appears in the show-ring other than as a member of a pack. He is only likely to be a household dog while being "puppy-walked" on behalf of an official pack of Foxhounds, but this does not mean to say that he cannot live his whole life as family dog.

A Foxhound may stand up to 64 cm (25 in) at the withers and is solid muscle and bone. He needs a great deal of food and is not fussy about the form in which it reaches his food-bowl. He disposes of the daily ration rapidly as behoves a dog that has for generations had to race his pack-mates.

A friendly dog, he adapts to life on a collar and lead very well. He can be taught civilized behaviour, but selection over the centuries to produce the ultimate fox-finder has also bred out those dogs that are not keen on the chase. An appearance in a high-standard obedience competition is unlikely.

There is also an American Foxhound, which is taller and lighter than the English version. It evolved from the first English pack that went to America in about 1650.

BREED BOX

Size	medium 64 cm (25 in), 30.5 kg (67 lb)
Grooming	minimal
Exercise	considerable
Feeding	has a very hearty appetite
Temperament	a friendly pack animal

GRAND BLEU DE GASCOIGNE

The Grand Bleu de Gascoigne is yet another native of France. He is best described as lanky as he stands up to 70 cm (27½ in). His devotees refer to him as having an aristocratic head-style, and his low-set, fine ears are long enough to sweep the ground and push scent into his nostrils while he is hunting his natural prey, the hare.

He is possessed of a deep, melancholy, baying voice. His coat is smooth and easily groomed. Black-mottled on a white base, it gives him an overall bluish tinge, hence his name.

With his obvious length of leg he is no slouch when he wants to run, but he has a reputation for lacking energy, not a characteristic which normally applies to a hound. He is a companionable dog, and he need not be costly to feed. Time will tell how popular he becomes.

♦ BELOW
In contrast with the traditional Foxhound, the Grand Bleu de Gascoigne is much narrower in head and body.

BREED BOX

Size	medium-large maximum 70 cm (27½ in), 32–35 kg (70½–77 lb)
Grooming	minimal
Exercise	necessary
Feeding	not excessive
Temperament	gentle and acceptable

GREYHOUND

The Greyhound is, of course, the template for what are collectively known as the sight hounds. There is a physical difference between those Greyhounds that course hares and those that are seen in the show-ring, but they all have the same instincts. The adult dogs retired from chasing the electric hare make wonderful family pets, but retain their instinct

to chase. This can well mean that they may not be popular if let off the lead in public parks while surrounded by other dogs. Fortunately, though, they are easy to clean up after a long ramble down muddy lanes.

◆ RIGHT
The Greyhound is the fundamental sight hound – lithe, muscular, deep-chested and tight-footed.

◆ LEFT
With a searchlight eye and unwavering gaze, the Greyhound is also known as a gaze hound.

They stand as much as 76 cm (30 in) high, and they can be surprisingly heavy for such a sleek dog. Their appetites are not excessive, but exercising them is fairly demanding if they have to be kept on a lead – owners need to be fit to walk fair distances each day.

A healthy Greyhound is beautifully proportioned and a fine sight, although as in all breeds of similar style, the pups go through a gawky, loose-limbed stage.

BREED BOX

Size	medium-large 71–76 cm (28–30 in), 36.5 kg (80½ lb)
Grooming	minimal
Exercise	essential
Feeding	medium
Temperament	affectionate and even-tempered

◆ LEFT
All colours – red, white and blue – are in favour. Anything goes as long as it is fast.

◆ RIGHT
The Greyhound is an ancient breed that may have originated in the Middle East.

HAMILTONSTOVARE

The Hamiltonstovare is alternatively known as the Swedish Foxhound. There is considerable similarity in type between this breed and the English Foxhound.

In his native country the Hamiltonstovare is a very popular hound indeed. He has a style of his own with the mixture of black on his back and neck, and his mainly rich

♦ BELOW LEFT
A white blaze down the centre of the skull and around the muzzle is the typical head-marking.

♦ BELOW
The Hamiltonstovare presents a wonderful contrast of colours in a classic pattern.

BREED BOX

Size	medium
	dog: 50–60 cm
	(19½–23½ in)
	bitch: 46–57 cm
	(18–22½ in)
	23–27 kg (59½ lb)
Grooming	easy
Exercise	necessary
Feeding	medium
Temperament	even-tempered

He has an appetite to go with his lifestyle, and he does not cause too much difficulty being cleaned up after a country ramble in mid-winter. He makes a thoroughly good canine companion for an energetic family.

brown head and legs. The white blaze on his head, down his neck, coupled with white paws and tail-tip make him instantly recognizable.

He stands around 57 cm (22½ in) at the withers, but he does not have quite as much body substance as the English version. He is a hunter with the same urgency in the chase as many other hounds; as such, he is truly a dog for the countryside, but he is very civilized if circumstances force him to become a temporary town-dweller.

♦ LEFT
Although the Hamiltonstovare is just that touch lighter framed than the English Foxhound, note the same classic white paws and tail-tip.

HARRIER

◆ BELOW
A good nose with well opened nostrils is
essential for this scent hound.

The Harrier is one of those breeds
that has been written about for
centuries. He is basically a hare-
hunter, and enthusiasts speak about
him as a specialist bred for the job.
The breed is rarely seen in Britain,
and no official standard is lodged
with the Kennel Club. In the United
States it is officially recognized,
but has no great show record.

BREED BOX	
Size	medium 48–53 cm (19–21 in), 22–27 kg (48½–59½ lb)
Grooming	easy
Exercise	necessary
Feeding	medium
Temperament	mild and kindly

◆ BELOW
A typical hound breed specifically selected
to chase the straight-running hare.

The Harrier stands in height
between the Beagle and the Foxhound
and in general terms has some of the
characteristics of both. Physically and
mentally he leans more toward the
Foxhound, as his whole inclination is
to hunt and chase. For anyone keen to
domesticate one of these dogs the best
advice is to resist the temptation.

◆ ABOVE
The origins of the old Harrier breed are
unknown, but today's dogs are thought to have
been derived from the English Foxhound by
selective breeding.

IBIZAN HOUND

◆ LEFT AND BELOW
The Ibizan Hound, with his characteristic
prick ears, has a restless energy and can
clear high fences from a standing start.

The Ibizan Hound, from the Balearic Islands of the Mediterranean, is typical of the hounds portrayed in ancient art on all manner of Egyptian scrolls and friezes. He will hunt anything, from squirrels to deer, tirelessly with scant

BREED BOX	
Size	medium 56–74 cm (22–29 in), 19–25 kg (42–55 lb)
Grooming	easy
Exercise	essential
Feeding	medium
Temperament	reserved and independent

regard for the imprecations of a frustrated owner.

A finely structured dog, he does not carry much flesh. He comes in varying mixtures of white, chestnut or tawny. His coat is usually smooth, but occasionally a rougher coat is seen, sometimes only in the form of a moustache or other facial hair, which gives him a very different, slightly amusing, appearance. In either coat he feels the cold and is unsuited to living outside.

He needs good, regular feeding to ensure at least a minimal layer of fat over his ribs is maintained.

SEGUGIO ITALIANO

The Segugio Italiano, also known as the Italian Hound, has been exported from his native Italy only in recent years and is not yet established in any numbers in other countries.

He stands some 59 cm (23 in) at his tallest, but there is considerable variation. He has a short coat that can be harsh or smooth, and in neither would he be difficult to groom. He is not a greedy feeder. His colour range includes black and tan and deep red through to cream.

He is generally lightly built with good musculature as befits an active hunter of considerable stamina. His temperament can be even, but early

◆ RIGHT
The length of ears is exaggerated with the same purpose as in the Bloodhound – to sweep scent up in front of the nostrils on the trail.

◆ ABOVE
The Segugio Italiano has a typically wiry body with the musculature to provide stamina.

BREED BOX	
Size	medium 52–58 cm (20½–23 in), 18–28 kg (39½–62 lb)
Grooming	undemanding
Exercise	necessary
Feeding	medium
Temperament	even

exports were not enthusiastic about being handled by strangers; things are reported to have improved, but it would still be advisable not to take one on without careful research among breeder enthusiasts, of whom there are nowadays a handful in most countries.

IRISH WOLFHOUND

The Irish Wolfhound is the largest breed of dog known, if not necessarily the heaviest. A magnificent creature, he is well proportioned even for a dog that may reach 86 cm (34 in) in height and weigh a minimum of 54.5 kg (120 lb). His expression of quiet authority and his rough, harsh coat give him a look of invincibility, while

◆ LEFT
This is the largest breed of dog, but there is no air of menace, even if those jaws are believed to have cleared Ireland of wolves.

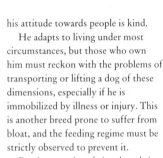

his attitude towards people is kind.

He adapts to living under most circumstances, but those who own him must reckon with the problems of transporting or lifting a dog of these dimensions, especially if he is immobilized by illness or injury. This is another breed prone to suffer from bloat, and the feeding regime must be strictly observed to prevent it.

Rearing puppies of giant breeds is a skill in itself, and the advice of an intelligent, caring breeder should be followed closely. Growth is rapid, but over-feeding can cause as many

BREED BOX	
Size:	giant
	dog: minimum
	79 cm (31 in),
	54.5 kg (120 lb)
	bitch: minimum
	71 cm (28 in)
	40.9 kg (90 lb)
Grooming:	regular
Exercise:	regular
Feeding:	very considerable
Temperament:	gently dignified

problems as too low an intake, as can any tendency to over-exercise during the Wolfhound's youth. In adulthood he will enjoy long rambles in the country, and he can achieve surprising speeds. The breed does not live to a ripe old age, but Irish Wolfhounds are such delightful dogs to live with that their devotees accept this with resignation.

◆ LEFT AND
ABOVE
This massive creature illustrates the range of chest and body sizes seen among the sight hounds.

NORWEGIAN LUNDEHUND

The Norwegian Lundehund, rare outside the Scandinavian countries, is a lightly built, spitz-type standing some 38 cm (15 in) high.

The Lundehund has a curious history. He comes from an island off the coast of Norway, and by a process of self-selection over the years he has developed the ability to climb cliffs so that he can raid puffins' nests for their eggs. This process of adaptation has resulted in him having six toes on each of his feet. The feet are turned slightly outwards, presumably to help the dog to climb the cliffs.

BREED BOX

Size	small
	38 cm (15 in)
Grooming	reasonable
Exercise	moderate
Feeding	simple
Temperament	alert and lively

◆ ABOVE
The Norwegian Lundehund's curious doubled dew-claw arrangement is particularly noticeable on the hind feet.

◆ LEFT
This attractive, though rare, breed has a gentle expression and a very appealing head.

PHARAOH HOUND

The Pharaoh Hound is surely the original Egyptian-style hound seen in temple friezes, albeit the breed now comes from Malta. A handsomely rich tan in colour with minimal white on his chest and extremities, he stands up to 56 cm (22 in) tall, not a large member of the sight-hound set by comparison with the Greyhound. This is a thoroughly tidy dog that has become reasonably popular since the early 1970s.

His short, smooth coat is extremely simple to groom but does not give much protection against the cold. He loves his exercise, is a superb mover, and is more likely to return on command than some hounds. In spite of his athleticism he is not a greedy dog.

BREED BOX

Size	medium
	20–25 kg (44–55 lb)
	dog: 56 cm (22 in)
	bitch: 53 cm (21 in)
Grooming	easy
Exercise	medium
Feeding	reasonable
Temperament	alert and intelligent

◆ LEFT
This could have come from the frieze of a temple in the Nile valley, so little has this breed altered in thousands of years.

◆ LEFT
He has the characteristic prick ears and light body of a Mediterranean hound, but the penetrating eyes show why this breed is one of the sight hounds.

OTTERHOUND

The Otterhound is a big-boned, shaggy dog that stands 67 cm (27 in) at the withers. He turns the scales at a minimum of 40 kg (88 lb), so he has a considerable presence. In 1978, after the hunting of otters became illegal in Britain, the breed was thrown a lifeline by the Kennel Club, which registered it as a separate breed. They have been

◆ LEFT
Otterhounds are no longer allowed to chase otters in Britain, so they plunge up and down rivers and streams after mink.

BREED BOX

Size	medium-large
	dog: 67 cm (27 in),
	40–52 kg (88–115 lb)
	bitch: 60 cm (24 in),
	45.5 kg (100 lb)
Grooming	fairly demanding
Exercise	essential
Feeding	considerable
Temperament	even-tempered

registered in the US since the early twentieth century.

Otterhounds seem to amble somewhat casually, and they give the impression of being extremely laid-back in their behaviour. Owners should have a love of exercise and a relaxed view about dogs bringing twigs, mud and the like into the kitchen after a family outing.

The Otterhound is a typical pack-hound in some ways, but unusual in being shaggy, massive and well attuned to the role of a house-dweller.

◆ BELOW
The Otterhound's imposing head has intelligent, gentle eyes, and jaws capable of a powerful grip on his prey.

◆ RIGHT
At his smartest the Otterhound is still not stylish, but his genial character and adaptability make him a good choice for an energetic family with space to spare.

RHODESIAN RIDGEBACK

+ BELOW
Rhodesian Ridgebacks are bold dogs that know no fear and have the physique to back that attitude.

The Rhodesian Ridgeback is a solidly built upstanding dog of considerable presence. He is characterized by a dagger-shaped ridge of hair along his back from his withers to just above his tail-root, which gives him his name.

In his native country he is a guard dog, and his height at close to 67 cm (26 in) coupled with a very solid frame make him extremely powerful. His

BREED BOX

Size	medium-large dog: 63–67 cm (25–26 in), 36.5 kg (80½ lb) bitch: 61–66 cm (24–26 in), 32 kg (70½ lb)
Grooming	simple
Exercise	necessary
Feeding	fairly demanding
Temperament	aloof and dignified

quarry as a hound includes lions, and his dignified bearing suggests that he would not flinch from the task.

Without a difficult coat to keep clean, he will appeal to those who want an impressive canine member of the household. Nobody in their right mind would contemplate breaking into a house in the knowledge that there was a Rhodesian lurking within.

He enjoys his exercise and his food; and he makes a handsome companion.

+ ABOVE LEFT
The Rhodesian's expression sometimes gives the impression of being able to hypnotize.

+ BELOW
While these puppies are charming, they will grow into large, powerful dogs. With their ancestry as hunters and guards, it may not be wise to choose one as a first dog or as a companion for small children.

SALUKI

The Saluki or Gazelle Hound is a dog of Middle Eastern origin. He is an elegant creature coming in a variety of colours, from white through cream and golden red to black and tan and

◆ RIGHT
The Saluki was much prized by the Arab sheikhs, who bred them as hunters to pursue wildlife over all manner of terrain.

BREED BOX

Size	medium
	dog: 58.4–71 cm
	(23–28 in), 24 kg
	(53 lb)
	bitch: 57 cm
	(22½ in), 19.5 kg
	(43 lb)
Grooming	essential
Exercise	demanding
Feeding	demanding
Temperament	very sensitive

◆ ABOVE
The Saluki is a sight hound, and those soft eyes are far-seeing.

tricolour. He sports a smoothly silky coat that carries longer feathering on the backs of his legs and also from the upper half of his ears. He stands as tall as 71 cm (28 in) at his withers, but he is lightly built, carrying very little fat – the dividing line between accepted and under-nourished is sometimes hard to assess. In spite of this he has great stamina in the chase.

His expression suggests he is looking into the distance, and he certainly has very acute sight. He is not a dog for a rough-and-tumble family as he is sensitive to loud voices and vigorous handling. He is admittedly highly strung, but his devotees rate him as extremely faithful to those whom he trusts.

◆ RIGHT
This is a lightly built breed in which speed is of the essence, hence those powerful thigh muscles. The feet are long, especially the middle toes, which makes the dog unusual.

SLOUGHI

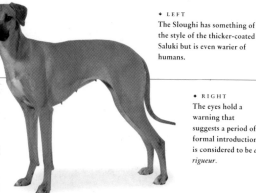

◆ LEFT
The Sloughi has something of
the style of the thicker-coated
Saluki but is even warier of
humans.

The Sloughi (pronounced "sloogi"),
from North Africa has been described
as a smooth-coated version of the
Saluki, but in fact he is a separate
breed, although of similar purpose and

◆ RIGHT
The eyes hold a
warning that
suggests a period of
formal introduction
is considered to be *de
rigueur*.

BREED BOX

Size	medium
	12.5–13.5 kg
	(27½–30 lb)
	dog: 70 cm (27½ in)
	bitch: 65 cm
	(25½ in)
Grooming	easy
Exercise	necessary
Feeding	undemanding
Temperament	indifferent to
	strangers

from the desert where he is known as
a tireless hunter.

This is another breed that has never
achieved great popularity. Most of
those seen outside their native lands
have not demonstrated the elegance
that they are reputed to exhibit. There
is a tendency to try to keep them lean
to a degree that suggests under-
nutrition.

Standing up to 70 cm (27½ in)
at the withers, the Sloughi varies
in colour from fawn through sable
to black with tan points. His
temperament with his owners is
affectionate, but he has little regard
for strangers. It would be as
well to make careful enquiries of
breeder experts before deciding
to own one.

WHIPPET

The Whippet has achieved great
popularity and justifiably so; he is
intelligent, beautiful, gentle and easy
to care for. Neat and tidy, with a
magnificent turn of speed for such a

BREED BOX

Size	small
	(27½–30 lb)
	12.5–13.5 kg
	dog: 47–51 cm
	(18½–20 in)
	bitch: 44–47 cm
	(17–18½ in)
Grooming	easy
Exercise	average
Feeding	undemanding
Temperament	gentle and
	affectionate

small dog – 51 cm (20 in)– he is built
on true sight-hound lines.

He walks close to his owner's heel,
hardly ever any distance away, whether
it is on a stroll down a country lane or
on a purposeful walk to the local
shops. He seems to fascinate all strata
of owners, and his amicable
temperament disguises his ability to
hunt superbly.

His coat is fine and close in texture,
and he comes in almost every colour
mixture imaginable, with a range from

◆ ABOVE
The Whippet is the smallest of
the true sight hounds and one of
the fastest movers.

solid colours to patches of all
descriptions. He does not cost the
earth to maintain, he is not a fussy
eater, and temperamentally he has few
equals as he seems to love people.

◆ LEFT
The Whippet, one of the most companionable
of all the hounds, comes in a great range of
colours.

The Gundog (Sporting) Group

Dogs from the Gundog Group (Sporting) are the most recognizable of all the breeds. The purpose of every breed in the group is to assist in hunting and retrieving game, be it furred or feathered.

Common points include their very easy-going temperaments (although there are slight variations) and the fact that they do not make much noise.

They range in size from the setters at 70 cm (27½ in) down to the Sussex Spaniel at 41 cm (16 in).

One characteristic that is seen in several breeds is that the strains that are most successful in the shooting-field are not necessarily very similar to those that find favour in the show-ring. It would be wise to ask the breeder about this if you are buying for a particular purpose. However, a high percentage of gundogs of every strain retain the intelligence and willingness to please for which they were originally selected.

◆ FACING PAGE **Pointer**

BRACCO ITALIANO

The Bracco Italiano originated in Italy in the early part of the eighteenth century. A mixture of hound and gundog (sporting), the original aim was to produce a pointing animal. In fact, today he is a multi-purpose dog and is used as a hunt, point and

◆ LEFT AND BELOW
The Bracco's lugubrious expression is the result of an original crossing of hound and gundog (sporting) types. This is a multi-purpose dog that will fetch and carry for as long as he is asked to do so.

BREED BOX

Size	medium-large 56–67 cm (22–26½ in), 25–40 kg (55–88 lb)
Grooming	easy
Exercise	necessary
Feeding	medium
Temperament	gentle

retrieve (HPR) breed. The Bracco Italiano arrived in Britain in very small numbers in the early 1990s, and Kennel Club registrations do not suggest that he is gaining in popularity. The same is true in other countries.

He measures around 67 cm (26½ in) at the tallest and has a fairly solid head and body. His fine glossy coat varies in colour from orange and white to red and white. He is an attractive looking dog and easy to clean up after a day's' work in the field. He is reasonably independent for a gundog, but he is nonetheless a good worker.

His suitability as a household or family dog remains unproven.

BRITTANY

The Brittany is a relatively recent emigrant from his native France. A lively, handy-sized breed, standing some 50 cm (19½ in), the Brittany is an HPR capable of carrying hare and pheasant.

He has a flat, dense coat with a slight wave, so he is not difficult to clean up. His distinctive colour is mainly white with orange, liver, black or tricolour mixed in. He is not expensive to feed, but he can be greedy so needs some rationing. Square-built, with a relatively short neck, his tail, which he wags enthusiastically, is usually docked short. He makes a cheerful, tractable family member and revels in exercise and work.

◆ LEFT
The Brittany is a superb setting and flushing dog as well as a retriever. It is a popular sporting breed in North America.

◆ ABOVE RIGHT
The Brittany comes in all sorts of colours and patterns.

BREED BOX

Size	small dog: 48–50 cm (19–19½ in), 15 kg (33 lb) bitch: 47–49 cm (18½–19 in), 13 kg (28½ lb)
Grooming	relatively easy
Exercise	essential
Feeding	undemanding
Temperament	energetic and busy

ENGLISH SETTER

The English Setter is a tall, handsome creature of comparatively slight build. He gives the impression that he knows he is attractive and intends to be noticed by all and sundry. As he stands 68 cm (27 in) tall, he is easily seen; he has a gloriously long, silky coat that can be a mixture of black, orange, lemon or liver with white. Like all such coats, it requires dedication to keep it clean after a day's work. The breed has a long, lean aristocratic head set on a long muscular neck.

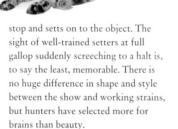

♦ LEFT AND FAR LEFT
The English Setter has, over the years, been bred in large numbers by top breeders who have produced their own very characteristic styles, but the soft eyes are obvious in all strains.

The English Setter can be trained to work in the field with speed and intensity, quartering large tracts in search of pheasant, partridge or grouse; once his relatively long nose recognizes an exciting scent he comes to a rapid stop and setts on to the object. The sight of well-trained setters at full gallop suddenly screeching to a halt is, to say the least, memorable. There is no huge difference in shape and style between the show and working strains, but hunters have selected more for brains than beauty.

As a family dog the English Setter is a natural because of his friendly nature; however, he has a wildish streak in his make-up, even if it is not as marked as in his Irish counterpart. He needs a firm, calm hand to turn him into a house-dog, and he is not ideally suited to life in the suburbs. That said, he has a host of urban-dwelling admirers who will disagree with this personal verdict.

BREED BOX	
Size	large dog: 65–68 cm (25½–27 in), 28.5 kg (63 lb) bitch: 61–65 cm (24–25½ in), 27 kg (59½ lb)
Grooming	demanding
Exercise	demanding
Feeding	reasonable
Temperament	a friendly enthusiast

♦ LEFT
The flecked colours in the coat are referred to as "belton", so you may have a lemon belton or an orange belton dog.

♦ ABOVE
A pose adopted by so many dogs when waiting for the owner to suggest a bit of action.

GERMAN SHORT-HAIRED POINTER

The German Short-haired Pointer (GSP) has only been seen in Britain since the early 1950s, but he has made himself the most popular of the dual-purpose dogs. A handsome,

BREED BOX	
Size	medium dog: 58–64 cm (23–25 in), 28.5 kg (63 lb) bitch: 53–59 cm (21–23 in), 24 kg (53 lb)
Grooming	easy
Exercise	essential
Feeding	medium
Temperament	highly trainable and friendly

◆ ABOVE AND LEFT
This is a true sporting dog, full of athleticism – smooth lines, tight muscles and an all-seeing expression.

powerfully made HPR worker, he allies a smooth, gleaming coat and a balanced, muscular frame with a keen nose and a high work-rate.

He stands as tall as 64 cm (25 in) at the withers and comes in variations of liver or black base, sometimes solid-coloured, more commonly with white ticking or spotting. The coat is short and coarse to the feel and is groomed with relative ease to keep its sheen. He has a squarish outline and his tail is customarily docked to a medium length. On the move, his muscles ripple with the style and grace of an athlete, and he requires regular exercise. He benefits from having his brain put to good use by extensive training, whether he remains a household member or finds his way to his intended role in the field. His is the sort of overall ability that it would be a pity to waste, as he is a genuine all-rounder.

GERMAN WIRE-HAIRED POINTER

The German Wire-haired Pointer, a more recent export than his Short-haired cousin, serves the same general purpose as an HPR breed. The two breeds differ not only in coat but in size, the Wire-haired being very slightly taller at 67 cm (26 in).

The outer coat is thick and harsh and the young, growing dog often

sports a moustache round his muzzle, which gives him a somewhat humorous look. The extra length of coat with a dense undercoat provides very good weatherproofing in the winter cold and enables the dog to be particularly good working in water to retrieve shot game.

There are not as many solid-coloured Wire-haireds as Short-haireds, especially in solid black, otherwise the colours are similar. Adequate exercise is vital as this is a working breed. These dogs do not enjoy being limited to a short stroll around the block.

BREED BOX	
Size	medium dog: 60–67 cm (23½–26 in), 25–34 kg (55–75 lb) bitch: 56–62 cm (22–24 in), 20.5–29 kg (45–64 lb)
Grooming	reasonable
Exercise	essential
Feeding	medium
Temperament	intelligent and biddable

◆ ABOVE
The GWP is heavier in body and limb than the Short-haired version.

◆ ABOVE RIGHT
The GWP is an HPR breed with a harsh, weatherproof coat.

GORDON SETTER

The Gordon Setter, from Scotland, is the heavyweight of the setter section. He stands 66 cm (26 in) tall, but he is more solidly built than any of the others. As a result he tends to move more steadily but still with considerable drive. He is a tireless worker who likes and needs his exercise; he does enjoy his food and can be heavy when fully grown.

He has a long silky textured coat of shining black with a pattern of chestnut-red tan on his muzzle and limbs. He grows slowly, as do all the setters, through a leggy, gawky stage, during which he can be the despair of his owner, but eventually he matures into a sound, dignified dog.

Grooming has to be thorough but is not over-demanding. This dog can make a good-natured companion as well as a reliable worker in the field and on the moors.

BREED BOX	
Size	large
	dog: 66 cm (26 in), 29.5 kg (65 lb)
	bitch: 63 cm (25 in), 25.5 kg (56 lb)
Grooming	reasonable
Exercise	reasonable
Feeding	fairly demanding
Temperament	dignified and bold

✦ TOP
Setters vary in style, but no-one can fail to recognize the solid build of the Gordon…

✦ LEFT
…or the particularly powerful head and neck.

✦ RIGHT
The Gordon may not have the glamour of his English and Irish cousins, but he is a trustworthy, steady, working dog and will last all day in the field.

HUNGARIAN VIZSLA

The Hungarian Vizsla (Vizsla) is a spectacularly coloured HPR breed from Central Europe. The short, dense coat of rich red russet only needs polishing with a cloth to keep it at its glorious best.

The breed stands up to 64 cm (25 in) at the withers and weighs some 28 kg (62 lb) and is strongly built with well-muscled limbs and a noble head that is not over-fleshed. The Vizsla is a worker with a great reputation in his

BREED BOX	
Size	medium
	20–30 kg (44–66 lb)
	dog: 57–6 cm
	(22½–25 in)
	bitch: 53–60 cm
	(21–23½ in)
Grooming	easy
Exercise	medium
Feeding	medium
Temperament	lively and fearless

◆ LEFT
There can be few more handsome heads than this – the Vizsla is keen-eyed and has an alert, intelligent expression.

◆ ABOVE
The sight of a Vizsla when the sun is at its zenith is a flash of the richest red.

native Hungary as both a pointer of game and a reliable retriever; he takes special delight in going into water in his quest for a shot bird. As a companion he is a good, affectionate

member of the household, but he can be fairly protective so he needs a firm hand. Easily trained by those who set their mind to it, he is a truly all-purpose dog.

HUNGARIAN WIRE-HAIRED VIZSLA

The Hungarian Wire-haired Vizsla is another HPR breed, very much like the Hungarian Vizsla, with the exception that the coat is harsh. He sports definite eyebrows, which give him a sterner expression. His height is

the same, as is his weight, and he demonstrates much the same characteristics of temperament. The coat on his legs is short and harsh and possibly makes his limbs appear larger.

◆ ABOVE RIGHT
The harsh coat is the same russet red as the Hungarian Vizsla

BREED BOX	
Size	medium
	20–30 kg (44–66 lb)
	dog: 57–64 cm
	(22½–25 in)
	bitch: 53–60 cm
	(21–23½ in)
Grooming	relatively easy
Exercise	medium
Feeding	medium
Temperament	lively and fearless

◆ LEFT
Developed in the 1930s, the Wire-haired Vizsla is a popular gundog in Canada.

IRISH RED AND WHITE SETTER

The Irish Red and White Setter comes as a surprise to those who have always recognized the traditional Irish Setter, often incorrectly called the Red Setter. In fact, the Red and White is reputed by the Irish to have been the original version, but he became practically unknown outside his native Ireland for almost all of the early part of the twentieth century.

◆ BELOW
Irish Setters are just red to most of us, but the original was probably this dog, often with more white than red.

His success since the start of the 1980s has been gradual as breeders have become more selective and people have begun to notice this handsome, large, red and white dog. He is similar in general appearance to the Irish Setter but has a slightly broader head and is more heavily built. He stands up to 65 cm (25½ in) at the withers and has a base colour of white with solid red patches on head and body and mottling on his limbs.

◆ ABOVE
These dogs have a characteristic brilliant white blaze down the top of the muzzle.

BREED BOX

Size	large dog: 65 cm (25½ in), 29.5 kg (65 lb) bitch: 61 cm (24 in), 25 kg (55 lb)
Grooming	demanding
Exercise	demanding
Feeding	reasonable
Temperament	cheerful and biddable

He does not eat greedily and enjoys human company. He makes a friendly family dog, but, like a number of breeds with finely textured, longish coats, needs careful attention to keep him clean and wholesome after a run in the country. He is not temperamentally as racy as the Irish Setter, but still can be quite a handful to control, and his training requires firmness and application on the part of his owners.

◆ RIGHT
The Irish Red and White Setter is a strong, athletic dog, good-natured and affectionate and deservedly growing in popularity, but it requires patience to train him.

IRISH SETTER

The Irish Setter is known to his friends as the Mad Irishman, with a devil-may-care way about him. He is certainly beautiful, but to keep that long, silky coat of deep chestnut gleaming requires thorough and regular grooming.

He stands around 65 cm (25½ in), but the official breed standard does not contain a height clause because, according to those who have bred him all their lives, a good Irish Setter cannot be a bad height. He is actually allowed to have a small amount of white on the front of his brisket, but nowhere else.

He does not carry a great deal of flesh, but his musculature has to be

◆ RIGHT
The Irish Setter first appeared in recognizable form in the early eighteenth century.

◆ RIGHT
Almond-shaped eyes with a soft, kindly expression characterize the Irish Setter.

powerful because he is expected to work at top speed in the shooting field. He is not expensive to feed, although he can burn up a lot of calories, and he expects to be well exercised. He can be trained to curb his wildness by those who set out to

be firm, and his attitude to one and all is of sheer friendship and *joie de vivre*. The recall exercise is not easily mastered by him.

The bitches of the breed tend to have very big litters of up to sixteen puppies at a time.

BREED BOX	
Size	large
	dog: 65 cm (25½ in),
	30.5 kg (67 lb)
	bitch: 26 kg (57½ lb)
Grooming	demanding
Exercise	demanding
Feeding	reasonable
Temperament	affectionate and racy

◆ RIGHT
The sheen on the deep chestnut coat is the reason why this is among the best known and most popular breeds in the world.

ITALIAN SPINONE

✦ LEFT
The Italian Spinone has recently arrived in North America, where the breed already has its devotees.

The Italian Spinone (pronounced "spin-o-ny") is yet another HPR breed that has entered Britain in the past twenty years. He stands up to 70 cm (27½ in) at the withers but weighs as much as 39 kg (82 lb).

He has a thick, wiry coat all over, and sports very distinctive eyebrows that are longer and stiffer than the rest of his hair. He also has softer hair round his cheeks and upper lips.

He can come in a variety of pastel shades of orange and brown on a white background. To complete the picture, he has a characteristic relaxed trot that appears tireless. He comes from areas where he meets both hilly terrain and marsh. His feet take a fair degree of pounding, but fortunately he is blessed with hard pads and hair between the toes. Dew-claws on all four feet tend to make his feet appear even more massive.

He has become amazingly popular in a relatively short time; his devotees speak well of his ability as an all-purpose gundog. They also rate him highly as a family companion.

BREED BOX	
Size	large
	dog: 60–70 cm
	(23½–27 in),
	34–39 kg (75–86 lb)
	bitch: 59–65 cm
	(23–25½ in),
	29–34 kg (64–75 lb)
Grooming	fairly demanding
Exercise	demanding
Feeding	reasonable
Temperament	friendly and alert

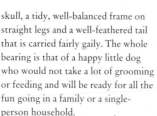

✦ ABOVE
A rough, tough all-purpose dog, the Italian Spinone's large hairy feet facilitate work in marshy terrain.

KOOIKERHONDJE

The diminutive Kooikerhondje from the Netherlands stands about 40 cm (16 in) tall and carries a medium-length coat with a slight wave in it, coloured with clear orange-red patches on a white background.

He has a kind expression, a sharply featured head with ears hanging close to the skull, a tidy, well-balanced frame on straight legs and a well-feathered tail that is carried fairly gaily. The whole bearing is that of a happy little dog who would not take a lot of grooming or feeding and will be ready for all the fun going in a family or a single-person household.

BREED BOX	
Size	small
	35–41 cm
	(14–16 in),
	9–11 kg (20–24 lb)
Grooming	simple
Exercise	medium
Feeding	reasonable
Temperament	friendly and alert

✦ ABOVE
Small and supple, the Kooikerhondje's active frame makes him a good candidate for agility training.

✦ FAR LEFT
The spectacular coloration and bushy tail helped the Kooikerhondje in his traditional role of luring ducks into netting traps.

LARGE MUNSTERLANDER

The large Munsterlander is a handsome HPR breed that originated in Germany. The dog stands 61 cm (24 in) at the withers. He is muscularly built and is similar in shape and style to the setters.

He sports a longish dense coat and has a fair amount of feathering on his legs and fur on his feet, which can get muddy. He is always a basic black with

+ RIGHT
The Large Munsterlander is a keen, all-purpose gundog with a good nose and excellent stamina.

a fair amount of white ticked with black on his body and limbs. His well-groomed coat has a glorious sheen to it when he stands in sunlight. He retains his full tail, which ends in a plume.

The Large Munsterlander enjoys exercise whether working or rambling with his family and, being a biddable sort of dog, he does not need quite the concentration required to handle a setter. This is a dog who can make a very pleasing companion for active folk.

+ RIGHT
This breed always has a black head, but the expression is alleviated by the gleam in those golden-brown eyes.

BREED BOX

Size	medium–large dog: 61 cm (24 in), 25–29 kg (55–64 lb) bitch: 59 cm (23 in), 35 kg (77 lb)
Grooming	reasonable
Exercise	reasonable
Feeding	reasonable
Temperament	affectionate and trustworthy

NOVA SCOTIA DUCK-TOLLING RETRIEVER

The Nova Scotia Duck-tolling Retriever comes as a surprise, if only because his name sounds highly improbable. This duck-toller does much the same job as the Dutch Kooikerhondje but uses a different method to trap susceptible ducks and other waterfowl. The constant waving

of their tails lures ducks near enough for hunters to shoot them, after which the dogs retrieve them.

The breed stands around 51 cm (20 in) and has a medium-length red

or orange coat with plenty of feathering, especially on the tail.

As the NSDR is blessed with a cheerful nature and enjoys being taught to be an all-round helper, he can make a good member of the household, but it remains to be seen whether his number will increase.

BREED BOX

Size	small 43–55 cm (17– 21½ in), 17–23 kg (37½–50½ lb)
Grooming	medium
Exercise	medium
Feeding	simple
Temperament	playful, trainable

+ ABOVE AND RIGHT
The main purpose of this spritely breed is to tempt waterfowl within range.

POINTER

The Pointer is instantly recognizable. The clean-cut lines of his lean frame covered by a short, shining coat make a beautiful silhouette on grouse moor and in city parks alike, although his whole purpose in life suits him better for the countryside.

At 69 cm (27 in) he is quite a tall dog. He does not carry much surplus flesh so gives the impression of being bony. His movements are fluent and athletic. He is not a big eater; he is very easy to clean up after a day's work, and he is

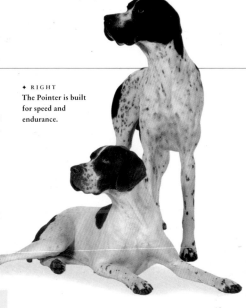

♦ RIGHT
The Pointer is built for speed and endurance.

♦ ABOVE
He uses his aristocratic nose to cover a great deal of moor or pasture remarkably rapidly.

BREED BOX	
Size	large
	dog: 63–69 cm
	(25–27 in),
	29.5 kg (65 lb)
	bitch: 61–66 cm
	(24–26 in),
	26 kg (57½ lb)
Grooming	minimal
Exercise	medium
Feeding	demanding
Temperament	kind and reasonably
	biddable

relatively easy to teach reasonable manners, though he is unlikely to win a top-standard obedience competition.

While most paintings depict him as white with a number of liver or black patches, he also comes in lemon and orange patterns. A kindly, gentle dog, he should appeal to the active owner.

♦ RIGHT
The Pointer was developed in Britain in the seventeenth century to find and point hares for Greyhounds to chase. Dogs of a similar type are thought to have been bred in Spain around the same time.

CHESAPEAKE BAY RETRIEVER

◆ RIGHT
The Chessie is a burly dog who delights in leaping into water, whether asked to or not.

The Chesapeake Bay Retriever is a strong, muscular dog. He stands 66 cm (26 in) high, which does not make him a giant among dogs by any means, but his purpose in life is retrieving ducks from his native Bay, which is usually cold. For this he needs much subcutaneous fat and a thick, oily-feeling coat, all of which add up to a look of substance.

He comes in a colour that is somewhat unromantically described as "dead grass" (straw to bracken). He can also be red-gold or brown.

His ability to work is prodigious. He loves people and is always ready to please, but he is not meant for the idle; rather for a family that enjoys the countryside and doesn't mind having a fair amount of it brought into the

◆ ABOVE
The head-shape is not that different from that of his Labrador cousin.

BREED BOX	
Size	large and solid dog: 58–66 cm (23–26 in), 31 kg (68 lb) bitch: 53–61 cm (21–24 in), 28 kg (62 lb)
Grooming	fairly demanding
Exercise	demanding but simple
Feeding	considerable
Temperament	alert and cheerful

house along with the dog. A very stiff brush and a chamois leather will repair the worst damage to his coat, but possibly not to the best carpet or the antique chairs!

◆ RIGHT
There's no getting away from the fact that, of all the basic retrieving dogs, this one is the heavyweight. His thick, oily coat protects him in the water and dries quickly.

CURLY COATED RETRIEVER

The Curly Coated Retriever is very obviously unusual in style as his body is covered with tight, crisp curls, even down the length of his tail. The only part of the dog with smooth hair is his face and muzzle. He is most often seen in black, but liver is not uncommon either.

His height is up to 69 cm (27 in), and he is well proportioned, so his powerful shoulders and loins do not make him appear clumsy or coarse. Those who employ him as a worker swear by his intelligence and ability in water, nosing out shot birds and bringing them to hand rapidly; he is noted for his prodigious shake.

He is energetic but not a greedy feeder. He makes a good guard for a retriever, is not hard to control and makes a good family dog.

♦ ABOVE
The coat is the mark of this calm, powerful water dog, with a mass of tight curls.

BREED BOX	
Size	large
	34kg (75 lb)
	dog: 69 cm (27 in)
	bitch: 63.5 cm
	(25 in)
Grooming	fairly demanding
Exercise	demanding but
	simple
Feeding	reasonable
Temperament	friendly, confident

♦ ABOVE
The aristocratically chiselled muzzle is smooth haired.

♦ RIGHT
It is thought that the Curly Coated Retriever originated in Britain as the result of crossing the now extinct English Water Spaniel with a retrieving setter and the later Lesser Newfoundland, which arrived in Britain in 1835 with the cod fishermen.

FLAT-COATED RETRIEVER

The Flat-coated Retriever is the lightest built of all the retrievers except the rare Nova Scotia Duck-toller. He is sociable and good-humoured, always eager to please. He is most commonly black, but there are a fair number of liver-coloured dogs. The odd yellow-coloured one is frowned on by enthusiasts.

◆ LEFT
The Flat-coated Retriever has a lighter body than other retriever breeds. He is a dog for the country rather than the town.

BREED BOX

Size	medium-large dog: 58–61 cm (23–24 in), 25–35 kg (55–77 lb) bitch: 56–59 cm (22–23 in), 25–34 kg (55–75 lb)
Grooming	medium
Exercise	medium
Feeding	medium
Temperament	kindly

Standing at most 61 cm (24 in) at the withers, he is not heavily built in the loins and hindquarters, hence his lighter appearance. His coat is dense and flat and positively shines with health after a good grooming. He is not a demanding dog to feed.

The Flat-coated Retriever is an excellent household dog who loves human company; his tail wags incessantly, and his intelligence is plain to see whether he is asked to work in the shooting field or play in the park.

◆ ABOVE
This retriever also has a less square foreface than others. His deep bark gives good warning of visitors or strangers.

◆ RIGHT
Flat coats originated in Britain as the result of crossing several other breeds, including the Lesser Newfoundland, and originally had wavy coats.

GOLDEN RETRIEVER

The Golden Retriever is a canine all-rounder. He can turn his talents to anything, from his natural retrieving to acting as a guide dog for the blind, a detector of drugs or explosives, a reasonably laid-back obedience worker or just being a most attractive member of a household.

He stands 61 cm (24 in) at his tallest but gives the impression of being a solid comfortable dog; he is inclined to get his snout into the trough as often as possible, and owners need to watch his waistline. There is often quite a difference in appearance between those retrievers used in the shooting field and the type that are bred for showing and the home.

The Golden Retriever has a dense undercoat with a flat wavy top-coat;

◆ LEFT
The Golden Retriever, one of the most popular dogs, is a wonderful all-purpose breed, although guarding is not his forte.

the colour varies from cream to a rich golden, which is sometimes very deep.

He is easy to train, but needs to be kept interested, because he is easily bored. His ability as a guide dog for the blind demonstrates his tempera-ment, as the work involves a great deal of steady, thoughtful walking.

He is one of the most popular household dogs because of his generous loving nature. Such popularity is often a curse because dogs are bred by people who are not always conscientious in their dedication to producing truly healthy stock. As is true of any breed of pedigree dog, the best source of supply is direct from a reputable breeder who has the welfare of the dogs he or she produces at heart.

BREED BOX	
Size	medium
	dog: 56–61 cm
	(22–24 in),
	34 kg (75 lb)
	bitch: 51–56 cm
	(20–22 in),
	29.5 kg (65 lb)
Grooming	fairly demanding
Exercise	demanding
Feeding	demanding
Temperament	intelligent and
	biddable

◆ ABOVE CENTRE
These dogs have generous soft muzzles that are able to carry shot birds, hares or even the newspaper without leaving a mark.

◆ RIGHT
The Golden Retriever was developed in Britain in the late nineteenth century.

LABRADOR RETRIEVER

The Labrador Retriever is instantly recognizable. Thought to have originated in Greenland, he is a stockily built dog; his coat is short and hard to the touch; it is entirely weatherproof and basically drip-dry. At one time the black coat was the best known, but yellow (not golden) became more widely seen fifty years or more ago. Today there is quite a trend for chocolate, which is also called liver.

The Labrador stands as high as 57 cm (22½ in), which is not very tall, but he is extremely solid. Another characteristic is his relatively short, thick-coated tail, which is known as an "otter" tail. Like the Golden Retriever he is a multi-talented dog, being much favoured as a guide dog for the blind. (In fact these two breeds are regularly cross-bred to utilize their combined skills.) He is also useful in drug-searching and has been used by the army as a canine mine-detector.

♦ LEFT
Labradors were brought into Britain in the nineteenth century by the Earl of Malmesbury to work the water meadows of his estate.

♦ ABOVE
Wisdom in a canine expression is difficult to define, but the true Labrador seems to get as near as any.

BREED BOX

Size	large dog: 56–57 cm (22–22½ in), 30.5 kg (67 lb) bitch: 54–56 cm (21–22 in), 28.5 kg (63 lb)
Grooming	easy
Exercise	demanding
Feeding	reasonable
Temperament	friendly and intelligent

Undoubtedly his greatest skill is as a retriever from water.

The Labrador seems capable of taking all the knocks of a rough-and-tumble family, which is why he rates so highly as a household member. His temperament is such that he does not seem to take offence at any insult.

He can consume any quantity of food so needs rationing if he is not to put on too much weight. He must have exercise and, although he can live in town surroundings, he should not be deprived of regular, long walks.

♦ RIGHT
With a frame like this, it is easy to see why the breed is famous for its stamina.

CLUMBER SPANIEL

The Clumber Spaniel may only stand around 42 cm (16½ in), but he is a lot of dog. Admittedly, he was never expected to rush around the fields in the manner of the Cocker or the Springer, but he has increased in weight over the years up to 36 kg (79½ lb) or even more and thus moves at a somewhat ponderous pace.

His temperament is kindly even if a trifle aloof at times, but he can be an attractive member of a household, though he should live in the country.

♦ ABOVE
These dogs will trundle through a day's shooting at a steady pace and never lose their cool.

BREED BOX	
Size	short but massive
	42–45.4 cm
	(16½–18 in)
	dog: 36 kg (79½ lb)
	bitch: 29.5 kg
	(65 lb)
Grooming	reasonable
Exercise	medium
Feeding	medium
Temperament	kind and reliable

♦ LEFT
A Clumber has loose skin on his forehead, and he suffers from drooping lower eyelids. Both of these things can cause veterinary problems.

His mainly white coat, with some lemon or orange marking, is close and silky in texture, but abundant in quantity. He is not difficult to groom. Despite his size, he is not a particularly greedy dog, but he does need exercise.

♦ RIGHT
The Clumber was bred at Clumber Park, Nottinghamshire, England, in the nineteenth century. He is thought to have originated in France and includes Basset Hound in his ancestry, hence the long back.

AMERICAN COCKER SPANIEL

◆ BELOW
Nobody could fail to remember a dog with a coat like this: just as well to keep the grooming requirements in mind before succumbing to the enormous charm of those eyes.

The American Cocker Spaniel is a derivation of the English Cocker Spaniel. In both countries, their own nationality is dropped in the official name of the breed.

The process of selection from the original stock has gone quite a long way. The American has a very different head-shape from the English; the muzzle is shorter and the skull is domed to the point of roundness, while the eyes are fuller and set to

BREED BOX

Size	small
	11–13 kg
	(24–28½ lb)
	dog: 36.5–39 cm
	(14½–15½ in)
	bitch: 33.5–36.5 cm
	(13–14½ in)
Grooming	extensive
Exercise	medium
Feeding	small
Temperament	cheerful and intelligent

look straight ahead. The other huge difference is in the coat, which is exaggeratedly long and profuse on the legs and abdomen. If left untrimmed, this coat is impractical for the working dog. As a member of a household, his coat is likely to present a regular problem if it is not kept well groomed. Prospective purchasers must take this into account. He comes in a whole range of very handsome colours, including black, black and tan, buff, parti-colour and tricolour.

◆ RIGHT
Note the characteristic peak to the hair over the eyebrows. This is one of the most popular breeds in the US.

◆ LEFT
These dogs were developed in the US in the nineteenth century to flush and retrieve quail and woodcock.

The American Cocker Spaniel is a thoroughly cheerful dog who does not eat ravenously. He enjoys his exercise, but is easily trained to behave in a suitable manner for suburbia. As he stands a mere 39 cm (15½ in) at his tallest, he does not need a mansion but will be happy to live in one if given the opportunity.

ENGLISH COCKER SPANIEL

The English Cocker Spaniel is the original of the American breed. He stands around the same height at 41 cm (16 in), but his coat is shorter and therefore nowhere near such hard work to keep well groomed, provided adequate attention is paid to his fairly hairy feet and his longish ears. He can

♦ RIGHT
The orange-roan colour is one of a huge range that this neat dog comes in. The breed is the basis of several of the land spaniels.

♦ LEFT
Low-slung ears with long hair make regular grooming a must.

be found in whole colours such as red (gold) and black, also in black and white, and in multicolours.

A thoroughly busy dog, he is always searching and bustling around

BREED BOX

Size	small
	12.5–14.5 kg
	(27½–32 lb)
	dog: 39–41 cm
	(15–16 in)
	bitch: 38–39 cm
	(15–15½ in)
Grooming	regular
Exercise	medium
Feeding	small
Temperament	merry, exuberant

in the grass and bushes. His name comes from his ability to flush out game, particularly the woodcock. He also delights in carrying things about whether on command or purely voluntarily. He is often portrayed as the original slipper-fetching dog by his master's fireside, tail wagging furiously.

♦ ABOVE
This dog shows a differently shaped eye, but still the gentle, relaxed expression.

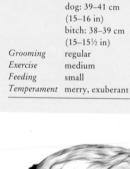

♦ LEFT
The Cocker's job is to flush ground game for his handler; the tight body is essential for his bustling way of moving.

ENGLISH SPRINGER SPANIEL

The English Springer Spaniel gets his name from his ability to flush birds rapidly into the air or "spring" them. A handsome dog, relatively tall for a spaniel at 51 cm (20 in), he covers much ground at a galloping pace. His coat is close and weather-resistant, and he is either liver and white or black and white. It is not hard to groom him as long as the hair round his ears is kept fairly trim.

He enjoys his food but is not greedy. He is a compulsive worker, apparently absolutely tireless. As a household companion he is similarly minded, expecting walks in either town or country, and he reckons that those walks should not be a mere stroll down to the shops. He is capable of learning all manner of games, preferably those requiring him to retrieve a ball – endlessly!

BREED BOX

Size	small-medium
	51 cm (20 in)
	dog: 21.5 kg
	(47½ lb)
	bitch: 19 kg (42 lb)
Grooming	reasonable
Exercise	demanding
Feeding	medium
Temperament	friendly and biddable

+ LEFT
The thoroughly balanced shape of the Springer means he moves rapidly and easily.

+ LEFT
The Springer has a charm that he is quite capable of using to his own ends.

FIELD SPANIEL

+ BELOW
Several breeds of dog are liver coloured – this one shows that gleaming colour at its best.

The Field Spaniel from England is easy to mistake for a Cocker with an over-long back. He stands around 46 cm (18 in) at the withers, and although he does come in black, liver or roan, the majority are a very definite liver colour. His coat is long, glossy and needs regular attention, especially around the ears.

He is a noble-looking dog, described as having rather grave eyes in his official Standard, and that is a reasonable description. He is active and biddable, making a worthy companion as a country dog, whether working or simply as a member of a household. He does not demand unreasonable quantities of food and deserves greater popularity.

+ LEFT
The Field Spaniel is a dog for the country-dwelling family – steady and trainable.

BREED BOX

Size	small
	46 cm (18 in),
	18–25 kg
	(39½–55 lb)
Grooming	reasonable
Exercise	medium
Feeding	small
Temperament	active and
	independent

IRISH WATER SPANIEL

◆ BELOW
This is a breed of great antiquity, although a clear type emerged in the nineteenth century from which today's dogs derive.

The Irish Water Spaniel is one for the connoisseur. He is tall by spaniel standards as he reaches 58 cm (23 in). The fact is that he is much more of a retriever than a spaniel. He is covered with tight liver-coloured ringlets, except for his muzzle, the front of his neck and the last two-thirds of his tail, which thus looks a bit like a whip. When he gets wet, his shake is spectacular.

◆ LEFT
The Irish Water Spaniel has a characteristic curly topknot of hair just above the eyes.

Aficionados regard him with great affection and enthusiasm and consider that he has a good sense of humour. He certainly is energetic, revelling in any amount of exercise whether he is asked to be a household companion or fulfil his traditional role.

BREED BOX

Size	medium
	dog: 53–58 cm
	(21–23 in),
	27 kg (60 lb)
	bitch: 51–56 cm
	(20–22 in),
	24 kg (53 lb)
Grooming	medium
Exercise	medium
Feeding	medium
Temperament	affectionate, if aloof

◆ BELOW
Grooming is no easy task, and the art must be acquired from the start.

Grooming him requires skill and knowledge of the correct technique, as well as determination. Feeding him is not a problem as he is not greedy. This is another breed that could achieve greater acclaim.

◆ LEFT
Another water retriever, the Standard Poodle, has played a significant part in the Irish Water Spaniel's ancestry.

53

SUSSEX SPANIEL

The Sussex Spaniel is another relatively unknown dog, but in fact is of considerable antiquity. The breed played a part in the foundations of the Field Spaniel. He stands at the most 41 cm (16 in) high, has a solid body and is possessed of a very handsome golden-liver coat.

♦ LEFT AND BELOW LEFT
This ancient breed of slow-working spaniel survived by the judicious use of other spaniel blood in breeding programmes earlier this century.

His head is somewhat broader in the skull than the Cocker, and his wrinkled brow gives him a serious look. He has massive bones for such a short-legged dog but does not need to compensate by being a greedy eater.

He makes a good member of a country household but has not yet become a family favourite.

BREED BOX	
Size	small 38–41 cm (15–16 in), 18–23 kg (39½–50½ lb)
Grooming	medium
Exercise	medium
Feeding	medium
Temperament	kindly

WELSH SPRINGER SPANIEL

The Welsh Springer Spaniel emulates the role of his English cousin. In fact the Welsh protest that theirs is the original version. The Welsh Springer is slightly smaller, standing 48 cm (19 in) high, and is not quite as heavily built.

He is an honest, kindly dog with a true will to please, easily trainable, thoroughly enjoys human contact, and is relatively easy to groom. He is not a dog that pesters for food.

He sports a glossy, flat and silky coat of a handsomely rich dark red and white. He delights in exercise and is a fine sight on the move. This breed has deservedly increased in popularity over recent decades and will certainly continue to do so.

♦ LEFT AND ABOVE RIGHT
For sheer beauty the sheen on the warm red of the Welsh Springer Spaniel's coat in summer sunshine takes a lot of beating. The kindly expression is a mark of the breed.

BREED BOX	
Size	small-medium 17 kg (37½ lb) dog: 48 cm (19 in) bitch: 46 cm (18 in)
Grooming	reasonable
Exercise	fairly demanding
Feeding	medium
Temperament	kindly and intelligent

WEIMARANER

The Weimaraner is an outstanding dog. He stands tall in the gundog group at 69 cm (27 in). A highly unusual colour, the Weimaraner is nicknamed the Grey Ghost though the grey can be slightly mousy rather than the silver-grey that experts crave. Possibly his most outstanding feature are his eyes, which can be either amber or blue in colour.

This is another HPR breed originating on the European mainland. His coat is short, smooth and sleek, although there is a rare version which sports a longer coat. In the more unusual coat he is no problem to groom – it is more a matter of polishing! Even when he spends a long day in the shooting field or on a country stroll through winter mud, he does not bring the outside world into his home.

The Weimaraner is not a big feeder, although he appreciates and needs a generously filled bowl on a cold winter's day. He does need exercise, because he has a temperament that requires plenty to occupy his very active mind. He can be trained fairly easily but does not suffer fools gladly.

He has a friendly attitude to people but will act as an impressive guard if his home or his family are threatened. He is not a fawning, easy-going type of dog, even if he comes from a group that appears generally placid.

◆ LEFT
The rare long-haired Weimaraner: note the undocked tail.

◆ BELOW
The truly stylish Grey Ghost is built on racy lines, but with the stamina and turn of speed which emulates the thoroughbred stayer of the horse world.

◆ LEFT
The Weimaraner's piercing eyes are a distinctive feature. Normally shades of amber or blue-grey, they may appear black when dilated with excitement.

BREED BOX

Size	medium-large dog: 61–69 cm (24–27 in), 27 kg (59½ lb) bitch: 56–64 cm (22–25 in), 22.5 kg (49½ lb)
Grooming	easy
Exercise	demanding
Feeding	medium
Temperament	fearless and friendly

The Terrier Group

The breeds that comprise the Terrier Group are the pest-controllers of the canine world, having been used originally to find and kill rodents of all shapes and sizes. They possess fairly similar temperaments; they have to be tenacious as well as sharp in movement and reaction. They are inclined to act first and think afterwards; they tend to argue with the dog next door and are not often the delivery man's best friend.

But a terrier which is properly introduced is a delight as far as humans are concerned. A family seeking an alert, playful, affectionate friend will be well satisfied with a member of this group. It may be thought to include one of the most popular of all dogs, the Jack Russell, although this is, in fact, a cross-breed and therefore not registered by either the British or American Kennel Club.

♦ FACING PAGE **Cairn Terrier**

AIREDALE TERRIER

The Airedale, from northern England, is the largest, by some degree, of the terriers. He is a splendid fellow, with a genuine style about him that entitles him to his nickname, King of the Terriers. He stands as tall as 61 cm (24 in) and has a head with an expression suggesting total command of any situation.

The Airedale is somewhat less aggressive towards other dogs than some breeds in the group, but will not back down if challenged. Few would dare! He is reputed to be intelligent but can be stubborn unless handled in a firm manner.

He has a black saddle and the rest of him is mostly tan; the tan can be a gloriously rich colour. His coat is harsh and dense and grows impressively but can be kept tidy with regular brushing. He sheds his coat twice a year, and at such times it is good for him to be trimmed or stripped by a professional. The experts will frown on the use of clippers, but it can be an alternative if he is destined to be a household companion and not a show-dog.

He makes a very good guard dog as he considers that his owner's property is his to look after. He has a loud voice that can be very convincing to any intruder. He is not a greedy feeder, but at the same time he is a well-built dog and naturally needs an adequate supply of nutrition.

◆ LEFT
These three youngsters will grow into king-sized terriers.

BREED BOX	
Size	medium
	21.5 kg (47½ lb)
	dog: 58–61 cm
	(23–24 in)
	bitch: 56–59cm
	(22–23 in)
Grooming	medium
Exercise	reasonable
Feeding	medium
Temperament	friendly and
	courageous

◆ ABOVE LEFT
The Airedale greets friends with a laughing expression on an impressively bearded face.

◆ LEFT
This splendidly elegant mature dog is ready to stand up to monster rat or human intruder alike. Although unable to go to ground, the Airedale displays all other terrier characteristics in abundance.

AUSTRALIAN TERRIER

The Australian Terrier is an alert, small dog. He stands a mere 25 cm (10 in), but there is a great deal of character packed into his small frame. His body shape is round rather than deep, but he has plenty of space for good lungs, which he needs in order to

◆ LEFT
The Australian Terrier delights in using his sharp bark to warn of a visitor's arrival; not often found in relaxed mood.

BREED BOX

Size	small 25 cm (10 in), 6.5kg (14 lb)
Grooming	reasonable
Exercise	not demanding
Feeding	small
Temperament	extroverted and friendly

be as active as he always seems to be.

He rates highly in his native land but has not yet achieved quite the same degree of popularity elsewhere. He has a relatively short top-coat, which is harsh in texture. This makes him easy to groom. He has an intelligent expression and carries his ears pricked.

He can have either steel blue on his saddle with tan on the rest of him, or an all-over red. Either way the Australian Terrier is a smart little dog who is surprisingly tractable and anxious to please. He can be very useful as a watch dog and can use his vocal chords effectively in the home. Being small, he does not cost much to feed.

BEDLINGTON TERRIER

The Bedlington Terrier is one of the most distinctive dogs of them all. Not only does he have a somewhat tucked-up loin, but he has an unusual coat, which is described as "linty". It is thick, with an unusual tendency to twist, and stands away from his skin. It needs regular tidying, which is

simple. The basic colour is blue or even sandy but most Bedlingtons appear off-white to those seeing them for the first time.

The breed hales from the northern areas of Britain, and its proper job is rabbit-chasing and catching. Nowadays

the Bedlington is also a very handy house-dog and pet. He does not have an enormous appetite, and he will find his own exercise given the chance.

His mild looks belie the fact that he is a genuine terrier in the best tradition of the group; underneath them he has considerable spirit.

BREED BOX

Size	small- medium 41 cm (16 in), 8–10.5 kg (18–23 lb)
Grooming	reasonably undemanding
Exercise	undemanding
Feeding	small
Temperament	mild

◆ RIGHT
A terrier in lamb's clothing, the Bedlington is full of courage in the house or as a rabbit catcher.

BORDER TERRIER

The Border Terrier is originally from the borders of England and Scotland and is popular as both a worker and a family dog. The fact that several veterinary surgeons own and breed Border Terriers speaks volumes for both their temperament and their freedom from problems. This is a friendly breed which appeals to many different people.

The maximum weight is just over 7 kg (15½ lb). This is a dog who is expected to work, however much he is adapted to living as a family companion. He fits that bill excellently. He has a cheeky otter-like

✦ RIGHT
The Border Terrier is described as "racy", which means giving the impression of speed without loss of substance.

head, a sound body clothed in a harsh, dense coat, and his legs will carry him across country or urban park for as long as his owner requires. The official Standard states that the dog should be

✦ BELOW LEFT
One of the most cheerful and companionable of all breeds, the Border Terrier makes an excellent family dog.

✦ BELOW
The Border Terrier has changed little since he first appeared in the late eighteenth century. He has found much favour in the show-ring but has still remained true to type. The Breed Standard describes him as having a head like an otter.

capable of following a horse, hence his sufficient length of leg. He is not quarrelsome, but he is game for anything. He likes being with people.

The Border Terrier comes in a variety of colours including red, wheaten, grizzle and tan or blue and tan; he is light enough to be picked up easily, and he does not require a great deal of food. He has a lot going for him!

BREED BOX	
Size	small
	dog: 30.5 cm
	(12 in), 6–7 kg
	(13–15½ lb)
	bitch: 28 cm (11 in),
	5–6.5 kg (11–14 lb)
Grooming	undemanding
Exercise	medium
Feeding	small
Temperament	game, friendly

BULL TERRIER

The Bull Terrier is certainly one of the odd dogs out in the terrier group. He is not a pure terrier – his name is a combination of bull and terrier – and, in fact, he was originally more a dog fighter than a small pest-controller.

The breed's shape contrasts with other terriers. The Bull Terrier is much more burly, he has an egg-

shaped head and a Roman nose. He gives the impression of being ready for anything and is nicknamed the Gladiator of the Terriers, a description that fits him perfectly.

The official Standard does not speak of measurements but the experts would accept around 45 cm (18 in) as reasonable, while 33 kg (73 lb) is no exaggeration of his weight. There is also a Miniature Bull Terrier, which is built on exactly the same lines but is not supposed to stand above 35.5 cm (14 in) in height.

The Bull Terrier is usually thought of as white, but even the white ones often have patches of red or black or brindle on their heads. He can also appear as black, red, fawn or brindle with a certain amount of white, mainly

on his head, neck or limbs.

His coat is short and flat with a feel of harshness about it. He is simple to groom, by sponging the dirt off and then rubbing him down with a cloth.

The Bull Terrier is a very active dog. He likes his exercise and food, and he is a grand dog to have about the home because he loves people, but woe betide any burglar!

The Pit Bull Terrier, originating in the United States, was also bred for fighting. As the result of deliberate training for illegal dog fighting he has been deemed dangerous and banned in many countries.

BREED BOX

Size	small–medium 45 cm (18 in), 33 kg (72 lb)
Grooming	easy
Exercise	medium
Feeding	medium
Temperament	even but obstinate

✦ FAR LEFT
The egg-shaped head of the modern Bull Terrier is hard as a bullet if the dog runs into you at speed.

✦ BELOW
There is no wasted space on this attractive, power-packed bitch – just solid quality in the flesh.

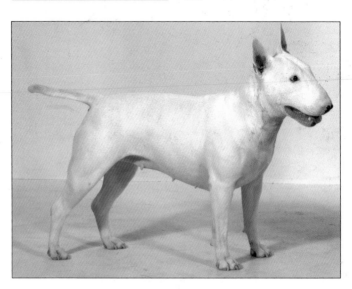

CAIRN TERRIER

◆ BELOW
Most Cairns carry more coat;
this one is in between coats, but
shows the neatness of line and
the reasonable length of leg.

The Cairn Terrier is an engaging creature, usually blessed with a fascinating character. Coming from the Highlands of Scotland, he is one of a group of breeds that are small in stature, large in heart. He stands a mere 31 cm (12½ in). His coat, which is harsh and weatherproof, can be anything from cream, through red or grey to almost black. The essential feature is that it should end up looking shaggy even after grooming.

His prick ears atop a small sharp-featured head give him a look of alert gameness, which is absolutely justified. He bustles everywhere at great pace, tending to catch unawares any small rodents that he chases. He is a tireless fellow, with an impressively sharp voice, who delights in accompanying his human family, be it on a country walk or a shopping foray.

He lives a long life, eats whatever he is offered and has a disposition that combines a devil-may-care attitude with a great love of people.

BREED BOX	
Size	small
	28–31 cm
	(11–12½ in),
	6–7.5 kg (13–16 lb)
Grooming	medium
Exercise	reasonable
Feeding	small
Temperament	fearless

CZESKY TERRIER

The Czesky (pronounced "cheski") originated in the Czech Republic. He is a kind dog with a coat colour varying from black through dark grey to a silvery look. Sociable and relatively obedient, he tends to be less aggressive than many of the other terriers.

He stands up to 35 cm (14 in) high and is slightly longer in the back than he is tall. His coat is not shed and needs trimming regularly with attention from brush and comb. He is not greedy but eats well. He enjoys exercise as a family companion.

◆ LEFT
The Czesky's traditional clip leaves a prominent beard and eyebrows, as well as long hair on the legs.

◆ ABOVE
The Czeskys were bred for underground burrowing work.

BREED BOX	
Size	small
	35 cm (14 in),
	5.5–8 kg (12–18 lb)
Grooming	medium
Exercise	reasonable
Feeding	medium–small
Temperament	cheerful, but
	reserved

DANDIE DINMONT

The Dandie Dinmont is another terrier whose appearance comes as something of a surprise. He has an expression that can only be described as soulful, with large round eyes peering out of an equally large head which is covered with what seems to be a huge soft cap or top-knot of hair. He comes in two distinct colours, a

◆ ABOVE
The Dandie Dinmont was named after one of Sir Walter Scott's characters.

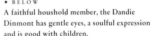

◆ LEFT
The Dandie Dinmont is more docile than other terriers but has a surprisingly deep and loud bark.

BREED BOX	
Size	small
	dog: 28 cm (11 in),
	10 kg (22 lb)
	bitch: 20.5 cm (8 in)
	8 kg (18 lb)
Grooming	medium
Exercise	reasonable
Feeding	small
Temperament	independent and
	affectionate

reddish brown through to fawn, which is dubbed mustard, and a bluish grey dubbed pepper.

He is longer in his body than he is high at the withers; he may weigh up to 10 kg (22 lb) so is not a heavy dog. He is also not a big eater. He thrives on human companionship and certainly makes an attractive household member. He never looks as if he would do anything in a hurry, but he can be roused to action by the sight of any rat or squirrel unwise enough to invade his territory.

◆ BELOW
A faithful household member, the Dandie Dinmont has gentle eyes, a soulful expression and is good with children.

SMOOTH FOX TERRIER

The Smooth Fox Terrier is a smart, alert dog. He stands about 38 cm (15 in) at the withers and always gives the impression of being right up on the tips of his toes. A lethargic dog of this breed would be most unusual. He is typical of all the square-built terriers, ready to stand his ground and argue with any dog who may challenge him, but not the one to start proceedings.

been very well schooled. He is easy to maintain in an urban area and will keep the rodent population down.

Grooming his basically white coat, with tan or black markings, is simple – use a stiff brush followed by a comb and finish off with a cloth. This regular routine will keep him looking very trim all his long life.

◆ LEFT
Most breeds of terrier came from somewhere in the British Isles; this one is the original hunt terrier used alongside packs of foxhounds.

BREED BOX	
Size	small–medium 39.5 cm (15½ in) dog: 7.5–8 kg (16½–17½ lb) bitch: 6.5–7.5 kg (14–16½ lb)
Grooming	undemanding
Exercise	medium
Feeding	medium
Temperament	friendly and fearless

The Smooth Fox Terrier will take all the exercise offered but will not spend his time nagging his owner to fetch his lead. He carries enough flesh to have a well-covered frame but does not run to fat unless over-fed and under-exercised. He is not a dog to leave loose near livestock unless he has

◆ RIGHT AND ABOVE RIGHT
The sharp outline and the way in which colour appears in distinct patches on an otherwise all-white dog is typical. This is a tough, no-nonsense breed.

WIRE FOX TERRIER

The Wire Fox Terrier is the rough-haired version of the Smooth Fox Terrier, with the same aptitude for rat-catching. He measures up to 39 cm (15½ in) and is square-built. His harsh wiry coat is white, usually with a black saddle and black or tan markings or a combination of the two. The coat grows thick and he should be trimmed fairly regularly. This is probably best done by a professional, but it is perfectly possible for an owner to learn the art, given a good teacher. Well trimmed, he is a very smart dog indeed.

✦ RIGHT
The Wire is the wire-
haired version of the
Smooth, with the
same balanced body,
short back and sharp
features.

BREED BOX

Size	small–medium
	39 cm (15½ in),
	8 kg (17½ lb)
Grooming	medium
Exercise	medium
Feeding	medium
Temperament	friendly and fearless

✦ ABOVE
The small, dark eyes are full of fire and
intelligence.

✦ LEFT
The Wire Fox Terrier is a bold dog who can be
noisy and wilful. He loves digging.

The Wire Fox Terrier is not a greedy dog and does not run to fat unless he is given insufficient exercise. A very good house-dog, he will guard his domain noisily. He imagines that his family is there purely to provide him with company and fun, whether they live in town or country.

✦ RIGHT
The breed is derived from
the old black-and-tan
Rough-haired Terrier of
Wales and northern
England.

IRISH TERRIER

The Irish Terrier is a handsome dog, standing up to 48 cm (19 in) at the withers; he sports a harsh and wiry coat of a sandy red colour, which may on occasion tend to be a paler wheaten tone. He gives the impression of being long in the leg, and he certainly is not burly of body.

As a result of not being thick-set, he does not need a lot of food to sustain his frame; he enjoys exercise, but this should be under strict control if there are likely to be other dogs about. He is a first-class dog for people of all ages and makes a fine house-dog.

His coat grows in a less bushy fashion than the Airedale's, and it is not hard to keep him looking neat, though he needs an occasional smartening trim by a professional groomer, unless his owner decides to take a course in the art.

BREED BOX

Size	medium
	dog: 48 cm (19 in),
	12 kg (26½ lb)
	bitch: 46 cm (18 in),
	11.5 kg (25 lb)
Grooming	medium
Exercise	medium
Feeding	medium
Temperament	good with people,
	fiery with dogs

♦ BELOW
The Irish Terrier, from southern Ireland, is one of the oldest of the terrier breeds. In the 1880s it was the fourth most popular breed in England. The Irish Terrier Club of America was founded in 1896.

♦ ABOVE LEFT
This dog bristles through and through with a love of action. He is still used as a working terrier in Ireland and is popular for field trials and lure coursing in the US.

♦ BELOW
Those handsome jaws contain one of the finest sets of teeth found in any dog.

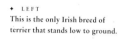

GLEN OF IMAAL TERRIER

The Glen of Imaal Terrier from Ireland is the shortest of the Irish terrier breeds. He stands roughly 36 cm (14 in) at the withers, and his back is long in proportion. His coat is wiry and not over-long. He comes in blue, brindle or wheaten.

The Glen of Imaal is a native of County Wicklow and has a roughness about him that disguises a surprisingly quiet dog for a terrier. He is not common even in his own homeland, but numbers have increased over the past decade. He is not a striking dog but has a happy, game way of going which makes him an attractive family companion dog.

He does not need a great deal of grooming, and he is not a greedy eater. He enjoys his exercise but does not expect excessive attention.

◆ LEFT
This is the only Irish breed of terrier that stands low to ground.

◆ BELOW
The Glen of Imaal has a surprisingly laid-back expression for a terrier.

BREED BOX

Size	small 35–36 cm (14 in), 16 kg (35 lb)
Grooming	medium
Exercise	medium
Feeding	medium
Temperament	game but docile

KERRY BLUE TERRIER

The Kerry Blue Terrier comes from Ireland. He starts life with a black coat, but this should change to blue in some eighteen months. It is a softer, silkier coat than is common on the average square-built terrier, said to resemble astrakhan, and it does not shed. He is normally kept trimmed to a strikingly neat outline, and this is considered a "must" by the devotees of the breed. The trimming should make him look as if he carries a neat beard.

He is tall for a terrier at 48 cm (19 in), and deeper and wider in the chest than the Irish Terrier. The Kerry Blue considers himself a superior being, and he requires a good helping of his daily food. He has a way of going when he is on his lead that is almost a strut, but he can go like the wind off it. He likes people and exercise; he is relatively easily trained but does not appreciate other dogs taking liberties.

◆ BELOW
Tall and powerful, the Kerry Blue acts as if he was born to be a champion, ready to take on the world at a moment's notice.

BREED BOX

Size	medium dog: 46–48 cm (18–19 in), 15–17 kg (33–37½ lb) bitch: 46 cm (18 in), 16 kg (35 lb)
Grooming	medium
Exercise	medium
Feeding	medium
Temperament	game

LAKELAND TERRIER

✦ RIGHT
This is a good working
terrier who nevertheless
makes a good family dog.

The Lakeland Terrier, from the Lake District of north-west England, is another of the group of square-built terriers. Standing 37 cm (14½ in) at the withers, he has a dense, harsh coat that can be all kinds of colours, from red through wheaten to liver, blue or black, with black and tan and blue and tan as alternatives.

Grooming him is not a huge task, but as his coat grows relatively thick, it would be wise to have him professionally trimmed every now and then or possibly learn to do the job yourself. In between, the use of an ordinary brush and comb will suffice.

He is an agile dog who loves freedom and exercise. A tireless working terrier, he delights in joining a family and taking part in any activity that is going on; and he is not over-noisy.

✦ RIGHT
The Lakeland
Terrier has
sufficient length
of leg to cover
rough terrain.

BREED BOX	
Size	small–medium
	37 cm (14½ in)
	dog: 7.5 kg (16½ lb)
	bitch: 7 kg (15½ kg)
Grooming	medium
Exercise	medium
Feeding	medium
Temperament	friendly and self-confident

MANCHESTER TERRIER

The Manchester Terrier is a fair height, 41 cm (16 in), and looks as if he has a bit of Whippet in his make-up. He is jet black and tan in colour and his coat is smooth, shining glossily after a good, hard polish with a cloth.

✦ LEFT
There is an
obvious
likeness in
this stylish
pair.

✦ ABOVE
This breed is well loved by
many devotees. With its
Whippet connection, it is
an unusual type for a
terrier.

He is a sporting sort who delights in family activity whether in town or country. He is not aggressive either to man or dog, and he makes a good companion for anyone who likes a dog to be a bit out of the ordinary.

He does not eat a great deal and might give the uninitiated the impression that he is a dilettante in his approach to life, but he was bred as a ratter and, given the chance in modern society, will prove he still retains his old skills.

BREED BOX	
Size	small–medium
	dog: 41 cm (16 in),
	8 kg (18 lb)
	bitch: 38 cm (15 in),
	7.5 kg (16½ lb)
Grooming	easy
Exercise	reasonably undemanding
Feeding	undemanding
Temperament	companionable and relatively quiet

NORFOLK AND NORWICH TERRIERS

♦ BELOW
Both Norfolk, here, and Norwich are small, solid terriers and great diggers.

The Norfolk Terrier and its older cousin, the Norwich Terrier, each bearing the name of its place of origin in England, are breeds of extremely similar type and style. They are eager, bustling, little dogs, low to the ground and thick-set in body. The essential difference is that the Norfolk Terrier's ears drop forward at the tip, whereas the Norwich Terrier's ears are pricked.

Their aim in life is to hustle foxes, badgers, rats, and anything that moves in the countryside, except farm animals and people. In fact, they are both capable of keeping their family companions on the move, but from in front rather than behind.

They stand a mere 25 cm (10 in) at the withers, with hard, wiry coats that tend to be rougher round neck and shoulders. The coat is red, wheaten, black and tan or grizzle, and it gives the impression that it is warm and thorn-proof. It does not present much of a problem when it comes to grooming, and after a country walk or a busy session down a handy hole, the coat is returned to its rough neatness very simply.

The two breeds are exhibited at shows separately in spite of the fact that there is little or no difference between them except the ear carriage. In either guise, aficionados have adopted the attitude that docking of the tail is optional, and more and more are being seen with this appendage left as nature decreed it.

Both terriers are good rough-and-tumble dogs with kindly personalities, who will not go round looking for a fight.

♦ ABOVE
There's a gleam in this Norfolk's eyes that speaks of fun and frolic.

BREED BOX	
Size	small 25 cm (10 in), 6.5 kg (14 lb)
Grooming	simple
Exercise	medium
Feeding	undemanding
Temperament	alert, friendly and fearless

♦ LEFT
This alert expression is the hallmark of the Norwich with its prick ears.

♦ BELOW
Wearing the look of a fun-loving breed, this is the Norwich at its sharpest.

PARSON JACK RUSSELL

The Parson Jack Russell Terrier is descended from the type of Fox Terrier favoured by a famous sporting parson from the West Country of England in the second half of the nineteenth century. Parson Jack developed what he considered to be the ideal hunt terrier, one that stood about 36 cm (14 in) and weighed in the region of 6.5 kg (14 lb), easy enough to carry on his saddle and capable of going to earth to bolt a hunted fox.

Devotees have continued to breed this size of terrier, which is quite different from the shorter-legged version, the popular Jack Russell seen in stable-yards, farmyards and family homes. The Jack Russell, which is a type rather than a pure breed, is a dimunitive rascal characterized by short and somewhat twisted forelegs.

The Parson comes in both smooth and rough coats, usually with a predominance of white with tan, lemon or black markings in the area of the head or the tail-root. These dogs make lively companions for lively households. They are easy to feed and groom, not difficult to teach good manners and view the human race with reasonable grace.

BREED BOX

Size	small-medium
	28–38 cm (11–15 in)
	5–8 kg (11–18 lb)
Grooming	undemanding
Exercise	medium
Feeding	medium
Temperament	cheerful, bold

♦ ABOVE
The Parson combines dedication as a worker with a playful nature. He makes a good house dog but requires plenty of exercise.

♦ BELOW
This is a balanced terrier; the rough-coated type is very much as the famous sporting parson bred it.

♦ ABOVE
These dogs have a sparkling eye and an intelligent-looking head.

SCOTTISH TERRIER

The Scottish Terrier has been popular
for many years but is not seen quite as
frequently as it was some fifty years
ago. He stands some 28 cm (11 in) at
the withers and gives the impression
of being a neat, powerful dog for his
size. He has a harsh, wiry and
weatherproof coat that benefits from
being kept tidy whether professionally
or otherwise.

The Scottie has fairly large prick ears
and carries a good deal of coat on his
longish muzzle in the form of a beard.

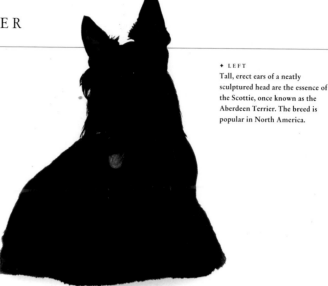

♦ LEFT

Tall, erect ears of a neatly
sculptured head are the essence of
the Scottie, once known as the
Aberdeen Terrier. The breed is
popular in North America.

♦ LEFT

The wealth of beard is another of the factors
that set him apart from the Cairn and West
Highland White Terriers.

♦ BELOW

Solid and thick-set, the Scottie is surprisingly
agile and active for such a short-legged dog.

BREED BOX

Size	small
	8.5–10.5 kg
	(19–23 lb)
	dog: 28 cm (11 in)
	bitch: 25.5 cm
	(10 in)
Grooming	medium
Exercise	undemanding
Feeding	reasonable
Temperament	bold and friendly

Most people would know him as black
or very dark brindle, but he does come
in wheaten as well on occasion. His
well-boned legs look almost thick-set
and his deep frame makes him appear
close to the ground. He moves with a
smooth level gait, as if he is very
important, and, though normally gentle,
is not a dog with which to pick a fight.

SEALYHAM TERRIER

The Sealyham Terrier is a small, sturdy terrier from rural Wales. He should not grow taller than 31 cm (12 in) at the withers, and the length of his body should be slightly greater.

He has a longer coat than some terriers, but it is also wiry. As it is basically white with small patches of lemon or badger usually on his head and ears, it is not simple to keep clean in the breed's natural country home,

◆ LEFT
The Sealyham is named after the Welsh village from which he originated. He has a marked independence of nature.

BREED BOX

Size	small
	31 cm (12 in)
	dog: 9 kg (20 lb)
	bitch: 8 kg (18 lb)
Grooming	medium
Exercise	undemanding
Feeding	reasonable
Temperament	alert and fearless

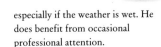

especially if the weather is wet. He does benefit from occasional professional attention.

The Sealyham can be a trifle cautious with strangers, but he is a superb companion or house-dog and a very effective alarm-raiser. He is known as a self-sufficient dog, who makes his own entertainment.

◆ ABOVE
The curtain of hair conceals a pair of very bright eyes that miss nothing.

◆ LEFT
A sturdy body on short legs tends to make it difficult to keep his coat clean, but the Sealyham does like living country-style.

SKYE TERRIER

The Skye Terrier has developed from the same root-stock as the Scottish Terrier. He is a very long dog, being only 26 cm (10 in) at the withers but twice that from stem to stern.

BREED BOX	
Size	small-medium dog: 25–26 cm (10 in), 11.5 kg (25 lb) bitch: 25 cm (10 in), 11 kg (24 lb)
Grooming	demanding
Exercise	medium
Feeding	medium
Temperament	distrustful of strangers

The coat is hard and straight as well as long, and covers his eyes. It needs constant attention, which can be demanding, so he is something of a specialist's dog. The Skye Terrier is cautious of those he does not know, while being very loyal to his own family. He is certainly a good watchdog and very striking to look at.

✦ ABOVE
Most Skyes have prick ears, gracefully fringed with hair.

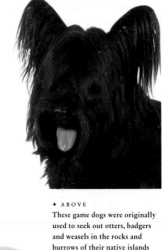

✦ BELOW
From contemporary records it seems that this long-haired dog with his flowing coat is much the same as he was nearly four centuries ago.

✦ ABOVE
These game dogs were originally used to seek out otters, badgers and weasels in the rocks and burrows of their native islands off the West coast of Scotland.

SOFT-COATED WHEATEN TERRIER

The Soft-coated Wheaten Terrier, as his name implies, sports a soft and silky coat that is always wheaten in colour. He stands up to 49 cm (19 in) at the withers. He came from Ireland originally, where he was a hunter, a guard, a herder and a companion to farmers. In 1943 he was registered with the Kennel Club in Britain, and in 1973 with the American Kennel Club. Today he is recognized as an attractive pure-bred dog.

He has a good-natured temperament: he loves people and seems to get on well with other dogs. He enjoys plenty of exercise, the rougher the better. In spite of the

length of his coat, it is not hard to keep in order. He needs as little trimming as possible, and he only eats enough to keep his prodigious energy levels up to par.

♦ LEFT
The breed retains its happy-go-lucky charm even in full show trim.

BREED BOX

Size	medium
	dog: 46–49 cm
	(18–19 in),
	16–20.5 kg
	(35–45 lb)
	bitch: 45.5 cm (18
	in), 16 kg (35 lb)
Grooming	medium
Exercise	medium
Feeding	medium
Temperament	good-natured and
	spirited

♦ ABOVE
It is hardly surprising that the breed is sometimes referred to affectionately as a "mop-head".

♦ RIGHT
This square-built, power-pack of a dog is full of confidence and humour. He makes a delightful companion.

STAFFORDSHIRE BULL TERRIER

♦ RIGHT
This solid boned and well-muscled dog was originally bred for fighting and ratting.

The Staffordshire Bull Terrier is not just a breed; it is a cult. The devotees of this smooth shiny-coated dog from central England often appear to be blind to the existence of any other sort. The breed is renowned for its courage, and certainly if any dog would be willing to defend owner and house to the death, this is the one. All he asks in return is adequate rations and a lot of love.

Officially the Staffie measures up to 41 cm (16 in) tall, but many bigger dogs are seen. His head is fairly big without being exaggerated. He views life as if it is entirely for his benefit. His body is built on the lines of a muscled midget, and he walks with a swagger – for prodigious distances if

invited. He can be groomed in a minute, not only because he is short-coated but brimming with vitality into the bargain. He comes in red, fawn, black or brindle with varying amounts of white. The colours can be predominantly in patches, sometimes over his eyes.

♦ FAR LEFT
The power of the Staffie should never be underestimated. In the company of other dogs or animals the Staffordshire Bull Terrier may need to be carefully controlled.

♦ BELOW
The Staffordshire Bull Terrier is a loyal and affectionate breed, with an ever-increasing following.

BREED BOX

Size	small–medium dog: 35.5–41 cm (14–16 in), 12.5–17 kg (27½–37½ lb) bitch: 35.5 cm (14 in), 11–15.5 kg (24–34 lb)
Grooming	easy
Exercise	medium
Feeding	medium
Temperament	fearless, dependable

WELSH TERRIER

The Welsh Terrier is a square-built breed from Wales, referred to by diehards as being built like a miniature Airedale, standing up to 39 cm (15½ in) tall. He has a coat of the same abundantly wiry type, and it requires the same professional care. He also comes with a similar black saddle and tan head and legs.

Perhaps slightly thicker set than the Lakeland, he has that breed's style of standing right up on his toes. He enjoys exercise; he delights in his family and all their occupations, including any form of game. Above all, he is as biddable as any in the Terrier Group, and he is not fussy over food.

BREED BOX	
Size	small-medium 39 cm (15½ in), 9–9.5 kg (20–21 lb)
Grooming	medium
Exercise	medium
Feeding	easy
Temperament	happy and fearless

◆ LEFT
This is an old breed that was originally known as the Old English Wire-haired Black and Tan Terrier. It is possible that the Welsh and the Lakeland Terriers have common ancestry from pre-Roman Britain.

◆ ABOVE
The set of the ears betokens intelligence and alertness.

◆ LEFT
Standing four-square on tight paws, this is a neat, cheerful, workmanlike dog and a good rat-catcher.

WEST HIGHLAND WHITE TERRIER

The West Highland White Terrier, or
"Westie", has pushed his way steadily up
the popularity charts, and this is no
wonder; he is a handy size to pick up and
carry when necessity requires it; he has an
outgoing manner; he loves people and,
though he will not buckle under when
challenged, he does not go out of his way
to pick a quarrel with other dogs.

He stands a mere 28 cm (11 in) at the
withers, but he packs a great deal of spirit
into his small frame. He is not as stocky as
the Scottish Terrier. As his name implies,
the Westie's coat is white and can get dirty
very easily; he therefore needs a regular
bath or a form of dry-cleaning with the
use of chalk. The coat is also harsh and
recovers its quality surprisingly quickly
after a shampoo, but Westies do need a
trim every now and then to keep them
looking neat.

He will use his sharp voice to warn off
strangers and so is a good guard. He
makes a great family friend or a
companion *par excellence* for someone
living on their own.

♦ ABOVE
The Westie shares common ancestry with the
Cairn. They were selectively bred to the white
by the Malcolm family of Poltalloch in
Argyleshire, Scotland.

♦ BELOW
The Westie has a merry expression and loves
company and attention. A devoted family
member, his small size will not prevent him
from protecting hearth and home.

BREED BOX

Size	small
	28 cm (11 in)
	dog: 8.5 kg (19 lb)
	bitch: 7.5 kg
	(16½ lb)
Grooming	medium
Exercise	undemanding
Feeding	easy
Temperament	active and friendly

♦ LEFT
The various
predecessors of today's
Westies were known as
Poltalloch, Roseneath,
White Scottish and
Little Skye. These were
merged under one
name, the West
Highland White
Terrier, in 1904.

The Utility (Non-Sporting) Group

The Utility (Non-Sporting) group includes dogs of all shapes, sizes and functions, from the Dalmatian and the Leonberger at the large end of the scale to the Tibetan Spaniel and the Lhasa Apso at the small.

There are two common explanations for the composition of the group. The first is that the breeds cannot be fitted into any of the other five groups, which is quite an unflattering way of looking at things. The second is that they are all companion dogs, which may sound politer but also suggests that the members of the other groups are not companions! To complicate matters, not all countries include the same breeds in this group. For example, the Japanese Akita is classed as a utility breed in Britain but as a working breed in the United States.

Looking through this section will undoubtedly give you some sympathy for those who had to solve the problem of how to classify such a varied assortment.

◆ FACING PAGE Schnauzer

BOSTON TERRIER

The Boston Terrier is a strikingly handsome dog. He is often described as the national dog of America, although his short muzzle confirms that he has Bulldog in his ancestry.

He stands around 38 cm (15 in) tall; he can vary considerably in weight around the 9 kg (20 lb) mark, but he is easily handled and picked up. His coat is short and shiny, and can be kept that way with the minimum of fuss. As his colour scheme requires brindle or black with white markings, he is instantly recognizable.

The Boston Terrier is compactly built with a square-shaped head and wide-set, intelligent eyes and prick ears. He is both dapper and boisterous, without being too short bodied; strong-willed but nevertheless a thoroughly good-natured house-dog.

◆ RIGHT
Today's Boston
Terriers are the
result of a cross
between the Bulldog
and the English
White Terrier (now
extinct).

◆ BELOW
Intelligence and
watchfulness are the
Boston's hallmarks.

BREED BOX

Size	small–medium lightweight: under 6.8 kg (15 lb) middleweight: 6.8–9 kg (15–20 lb) heavyweight: 9–11.3 kg (20–25 lb)
Grooming	simple
Exercise	undemanding
Feeding	undemanding
Temperament	determined

◆ LEFT
Boston Terriers were
originally bigger and
heavier, but careful
selective breeding
has produced the
clean-cut dog of
today.

◆ ABOVE
The Boston Terrier has a characteristically
short muzzle and a square head.

BULLDOG

◆ LEFT
Affectionately nicknamed "Old Sourmug", the Bulldog's face is definitely his fortune because of his uncompromisingly upturned chin.

The Bulldog, often referred to as the British Bulldog to distinguish him from any other, is instantly recognized by all who see him.

He has a friendly, if stubborn nature. His devotees will not hear a word against him, but those who fancy taking one on must understand his special needs. His physical characteristics, for example, mean that a walk should not be conducted at a

giving the impression that his muscles have been built up like those of a human weight-lifter. He weighs 25 kg (55 lb), sometimes more, and he eats as befits his size. He is a superb guard dog and he adores children. He is reasonably good with other dogs as he simply appears to ignore them; but he can give a show of aggression towards strangers, human or canine, if provoked.

BREED BOX

Size	small-medium dog: 25 kg (55 lb) bitch: 22.5 kg (50 lb)
Grooming	simple
Exercise	undemanding
Feeding	medium
Temperament	affectionate and determined

◆ BELOW AND FAR LEFT
The Bulldog today is radically different from the bull fighting dog of old. The ferocity and viciousness have been bred out.

great pace, especially in the heat of the day. The shape of his head and his breathing apparatus mean that he can easily become short of breath; he can, on occasion, put in a surprising burst of speed, but over-exertion on a hot day can, and does, have serious side-effects. In addition, he tends to breathe noisily.

The Bulldog was bred to get to grips with bulls by grabbing their noses with his front teeth. The design of jaw for which he was bred, in the days when bull-baiting was legal, has been considerably exaggerated in recent times, even though it is no longer necessary to fulfil that role.

His coat is short and easily kept clean; he can be all manner of colours from red through fawn to white or pied. He is a massively built dog,

CANAAN DOG

♦ LEFT AND BELOW
Two very alert puppies of a breed that is new to western civilization, and a typically watchful adult.

The Canaan Dog is a relatively recent export from the deserts of the Middle East, hailing predominantly from Israel. He retains much of the semi-wild and has yet to settle into modern western society. He is a true canine athlete standing up to 61 cm (24½ in) at the withers and is built on the lines of a racing hunter rather than a heavy plodder, so he is not a greedy dog.

His coat, which is of medium length, is easily groomed; it ranges in colour from red to sand or may be either black or white. He has good guarding instincts as well as those of the hunter. He is one of the anomalies in the Utility Group, being more of a Working dog in his lifestyle.

The Canaan Dog's origins indicate that he needs plenty of exercise and likes his freedom; he is versatile but needs time to prove his adaptability to western concepts of obedience.

BREED BOX	
Size	medium–large 51–61 cm (20–24 in), 18–25 kg (39½–55lb)
Grooming	undemanding
Exercise	demanding
Feeding	medium
Temperament	alert and distrustful of strangers

CHOW CHOW

♦ BELOW LEFT
The Chow Chow is a distinctive Chinese breed with a scowling expression and upright gait.

The Chow Chow is an example of a spitz breed, with his square-built frame, tightly curled tail and prick ears. He is unusual in that he has a very laid-back temperament, seldom rousing himself to move at any considerable speed. His movement is stilted and stiff-legged. The inside of his mouth and his tongue are black.

He stands up to 56 cm (22 in) at his tallest, and he is thick-set in body. He does not eat heartily considering his apparent bulk, but this is partly exaggerated by the thickness of his very plush coat, which can be black, red, blue, fawn or cream. It is not an easy coat to groom effectively and requires regular attention.

The Chow Chow originated in China, where he performed all kinds of functions, from guarding and companionship right through to ending up as a possible source of food for humans! He is a loyal dog to his owners but does not respond well to strangers. At one time he was considered bad-tempered. Nevertheless, he attracts a host of admirers, but he does need careful attention from those who do not know the breed well.

BREED BOX	
Size	small–medium dog: 48–56 cm (19–22 in), 27 kg (59½ lb) bitch: 46–51 cm (18–20 in), 25 kg (55 lb)
Grooming	demanding
Exercise	undemanding
Feeding	medium
Temperament	independent but loyal

DALMATIAN

The Dalmatian is as distinctive a breed as any. With his white base colour and plethora of spots, either black or liver, all over his head, body and limbs, he is the original "spotted dog". He has been known in Britain for well over a century and was originally used as a carriage dog; he has a penchant for

running between the wheels, quite undaunted by the close proximity of flashing hooves. In the US he was used to control the horses that pulled fire appliances and is still a well-known fire house mascot.

The Dalmatian is a handsome dog up to 61 cm (24 in) in Britain, 58.5 cm (23 in) in the US. He could

not be more friendly to people. He lives to a ripe old age and never seems to slow down. He loves running and needs plenty of exercise, so owners need to be fit. His coat, being short, is no problem to groom, and in spite of his size he does not overeat.

◆ **LEFT**
The essence of the Dalmatian is that no part of the dog is ever still, especially that long, tapering tail.

◆ **BELOW FAR LEFT**
This is a dog of ancient ancestry and uncertain origins. The first undisputed record of him is in Dalmatia, on the Adriatic coast; hence his name.

◆ **BELOW**
These dogs are always ready for the next walk.

◆ **BELOW**
This bitch is a youngster, a full-grown dog can be a handful to control.

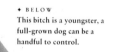

BREED BOX

Size	large dog: 58.5–61 cm (23–24 in), 27 kg (60 lb) bitch: 56–58.5 cm (22–23 in), 25 kg (55 lb)
Grooming	easy
Exercise	demanding
Feeding	medium
Temperament	outgoing and friendly

FRENCH BULLDOG

The French Bulldog is the French version of the British Bulldog. He has a similar square face but without the exaggeration of the shortened muzzle. He carries his large ears erect, well-up on his skull. His dark eyes are full of expression, usually kindly but capable of a glint which suggests that he does not suffer fools gladly.

◆ LEFT
French Bulldogs can move very much faster than their solid frame might suggest.

He can weigh up to 12.5 kg (27½ lb) but enjoys his food, so his diet must be controlled. He comes in dark brindle, fawn or pied, and his coat is short, close and shiny, so easily

◆ ABOVE
The large upright ears tend to swivel to pick up every sound.

groomed. He is compactly built with a slight concave curve over his loins, and like his British cousin he has a short tail, which can be corkscrew-shaped.

He rushes about when taking exercise, but finds hot days hard going, tending to breathe noisily when under severe stress. He makes a charming house-dog and gives the impression that he would guard hearth and home with his life.

◆ ABOVE
These dogs both have pied coloration; the most desired pattern comes with a neat central band down the forehead.

◆ LEFT
French Bulldogs are one of the few breeds that have their loins higher than their withers; this helps them to launch themselves vertically, as if on springs.

BREED BOX	
Size	small-medium 30.5–31.5 cm (12–12½ in) dog: 12.5 kg (27½ lb) bitch: 11 kg (24 lb)
Grooming	easy
Exercise	undemanding
Feeding	undemanding
Temperament	cheerful and intelligent

GERMAN SPITZ

The German Spitz has two recognized varieties in two different sizes. In its country of origin there are, in fact, five different sizes ranging from the Wolfspitz, which stands around 53 cm (21 in) to the Pomeranian, which is the smallest at less than 20 cm (8 in).

The two recognized varieties are the middle size and the next size down, officially christened the German Spitz (Mittel), measuring between 30 and 38 cm (12–15 in), and the German Spitz (Klein) measuring 23–29 cm (9–11½ in).

Apart from the size variation the Mittel and the Klein are identical; they are prick-eared, sharp-featured dogs with compact bodies and tightly

◆ ABOVE
A pair of perky Kleins with intelligent eyes and good bone structure.

◆ LEFT
No matter which size, a German Spitz carries a great deal of coat which needs a great deal of grooming. This one is a Mittel.

◆ RIGHT
A typical spitz head.

curled tails. They have thick, harsh-textured coats that keep them warm in the coldest of winters. They come in every variety of colour, from chocolate to white, as well as in all sorts of combinations. Their coats look marvellous after a thorough grooming, but they are not for the lazy owner.

They are sturdy, cheerful creatures, capable of raising a merry chorus to warn of the arrival of a stranger but delighted when the stranger turns out to be a friend. They will join in all the family fun and make good companions for all ages.

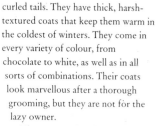

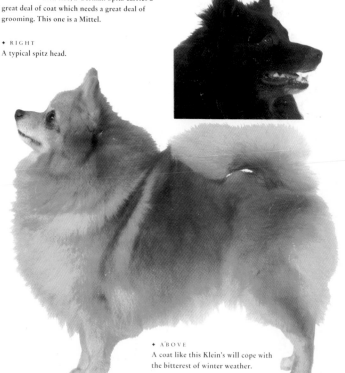

◆ ABOVE
A coat like this Klein's will cope with the bitterest of winter weather.

BREED BOX

Size	small
	Mittel: 30–38 cm
	(12–15 in),
	10.5–11.5 kg
	(23–25 lb)
	Klein: 23–29 cm
	(9–11½), 8–10 kg
	(17½–22 lb)
Grooming	demanding
Exercise	medium
Feeding	undemanding
Temperament	happy and lively

JAPANESE AKITA

♦ ABOVE
The Japanese Akita comes in
a series of very striking
colours and patterns.

The Japanese Akita, or simply Akita, is included in the working group by some countries. The Japanese Akita is striking; no other word fits such a powerfully built dog. He stands up to 71 cm (28 in) at the withers and his legs and body are designed on lines that would do credit to a champion bull. The Japanese bred him as a fighting dog, and his temperament, certainly among the males, is often awesome and need to be watched.

He attracts people with his brilliant colour schemes, which range from white through brindle and pinto to grey. Whatever colour he is, his thick, plush coat shines. That coat needs grooming to bring out the best in it. The typical spitz shape of pricked ears, which are hooded, wedge-shaped head, taut, compact body and curled tail are all there in the dog, but in no other spitz breed are they so expressive. He needs a lot of exercise as he is all muscle; he needs control as he is bossy and very intelligent; he needs feeding to go with his bulk but is not greedy. He is not always an ideal family dog.

If he is the dog that fits the lifestyle, he is superb. Rather than asking, "Is this the dog for me?" the question should be, "Am I the person for the dog?"

BREED BOX	
Size	large
	50 kg (110 lb)
	dog: 66–71 cm
	(26–28 in)
	bitch: 62–66 cm
	(24½ –26 in)
Grooming	medium
Exercise	demanding
Feeding	medium
Temperament	courageous and
	dominating

JAPANESE SHIBA INU

♦ ABOVE
The Shiba Inu is the smallest of the Japanese
breeds and of ancient origin.

The Japanese Shiba Inu (Shiba Inu) stands up to 39.5 cm (15½ in). He is much the same shape as the Akita, including the hooded ears that tip sightly forward continuing the topline of his neck. He has the same plush feel to the coat, but comes in less striking colours, including red, black, black and tan, and brindle, which do not have quite the same brilliance.

His temperament is not so dominating, though his intelligence is just as obvious; a Shiba will think his way through to getting what he wants. He is not noisy but will spot the invader of his owner's property without making a scene about it.

He loves his family and joining in all activities, but he is not a restlessly demanding dog. He is trainable and enjoys learning.

♦ LEFT
The Shiba Inu's plush coat comes in a
variety of colours. Note the hooded ears.

BREED BOX	
Size	small
	8–10 kg (18–22 lb)
	dog: 39.5 cm (15½ in)
	bitch: 36.5 cm
	(14 in)
Grooming	reasonable
Exercise	reasonable
Feeding	reasonable
Temperament	bright and
	intelligent

JAPANESE SPITZ

The Japanese Spitz arrived in Europe less than twenty years ago but is already well established. Standing about 36 cm (14 in) tall, he is a neat, sharply outlined dog with a stand-off coat that is never anything but

BREED BOX

Size	small
	30–36 cm
	(12–14 in),
	5–6 kg (11–13 lb)
Grooming	medium
Exercise	medium
Feeding	undemanding
Temperament	affectionate and
	alert

✦ ABOVE
The pointed muzzle should be neither too thick nor too long.

brilliant white. Considering the thickness of his coat, he is not too difficult to groom or even to keep clean, although it will obviously need regular attention.

He is not over-noisy indoors or out, but makes a good sentry. He is capable of being an extremely companionable and nimble character whether with a large family or a single householder. He is not greedy but is not a picky feeder for what, at first sight, looks like a dainty dog.

✦ BELOW
Three delightful Japanese Spitz, with their coats gleaming like freshly fallen snow. It's possible that these small, nimble dogs have the same ancestry as the Samoyeds.

KEESHOND

The Keeshond comes from Holland, where he guards farms and barges, and is also known as the Dutch Barge Dog. He is another spitz with smallish pricked ears, a compact body and the most tightly curled tail of all the spitzes. He stands around 46 cm (18 in) and is solidly built; he can be a greedy feeder and needs rationing if he is not to put on excess weight.

His harsh coat is thick, and he comes in what is officially called silver-grey – in fact, he sports long guard-hairs that have black tips. He withstands freezing temperatures and snow, regarding them with contempt, and considers central heating in his owner's house to be a sign of weakness! Grooming him is hard work, but his is the sort of coat that well rewards those who are conscientious and dedicated.

He loves human company and the exercise which goes with a busy family, but he is not demanding. He has sharp hearing and responds noisily to the arrival of visitors or the intrusion of strangers.

♦ LEFT
The Keeshond is a very solidly built, hardy dog that can live happily in the toughest of weather conditions. He was used as a guard and vermin catcher in his native Holland.

♦ BELOW
Thoroughly trusting and cheerful, the Keeshond loves people.

BREED BOX	
Size	small–medium
	dog: 46 cm (18 in),
	19.5 kg (43 lb)
	bitch: 43 cm (17 in),
	18 kg (39½ lb)
Grooming	demanding
Exercise	medium
Feeding	medium
Temperament	friendly and
	vociferous

♦ LEFT
The coat does not look like this one unless someone has made a great effort.

LEONBERGER

Make no mistake, the Leonberger is a whole lot of dog: he can stand as tall as 80 cm (32 in). He derives from the town of Leonberg in Germany, and he has traces of several large breeds in his

♦ LEFT
His size means he is not really suited to town or flat dwelling.

ancestry. As could be expected from his bulk, he needs a great deal of feeding to sustain him.

His inclusion in the Utility Group is questionable because he has far more in common with members of the Working Group. He is a friendly dog, but he can give a good account of himself if asked to guard his home. His coat is

of medium length and is not all that hard to groom except there is so much of it. The colour range is from reddish brown through golden to a lighter yellow, but most specimens have a black mask on their cheerful faces.

His attitude to exercise reflects his attitude to life and people. He is accommodating and easygoing. He does not see much point in hurrying anywhere, preferring to amble amiably. He is also a good swimmer in any weather and, given his size, is best suited to country life. He is first and foremost an easy, genial companion.

♦ ABOVE
The closer you get to a Leonberger the kinder the expression.

♦ BELOW
Leonbergers move deliberately, with a long-striding gait, and a great deal faster than their size might suggest.

BREED BOX	
Size	very large
	34–50 kg
	(75–110 lb)
	dog: 72–80 cm
	(28–32 in)
	bitch: 65–75 cm
	(25½ –29½ in)
Grooming	fairly demanding
Exercise	medium
Feeding	demanding
Temperament	kindly

LHASA APSO

The Lhasa Apso is a native of Tibet, where these dogs were originally kept as indoor guards. With their intelligence and sharp hearing, they were ideally suited to the task. Their long, hard coats protected them from the severities of the climate. These days a Lhasa Apso can be glamour personified, the colour of the coat ranging from gold to grey, but that show-ring gleam is not achieved without regular shampoos and lots of hard work.

The Lhasa Apso stands around the 25 cm (10 in) mark at his withers, but he sports a back that is a little bit longer than his height, though not so exaggeratedly as to make him prone to a weakened spine. His appetite is appropriate to his small size.

His head, under all the hair that often covers his face, is much more like that of one of the smaller terriers than one would expect. He is tough in cold weather, and he will cheerfully walk for miles. He has an independent nature and is wary of strangers, although very affectionate with his owners. He makes a delightful family companion.

✦ ABOVE
The long hair falling over the Lhasa Apsos' eyes protected them from the wind and glare in their native Tibet.

BREED BOX	
Size	small 25–28 cm (10–11 in), 6–7 kg (13–15½ lb)
Grooming	demanding
Exercise	undemanding
Feeding	undemanding
Temperament	companionable but haughty

✦ ABOVE LEFT
With the hair swept back from the eyes, the Lhasa Apso has a soulful expression.

✦ LEFT
Lhasa Apsos must be seen on the move to realize just how active the dog under that mass of coat really is.

MINIATURE SCHNAUZER

The Miniature Schnauzer (Terrier Group), one of three Schnauzer breeds, gives the impression that he should be banded together with the square-built members of the Terrier Group, which indeed he is in the US. Standing around 36 cm (14 in) in a coat that is harsh and wiry, his must be one of the most stylish outlines of any dog.

To achieve the look that you see in the show-ring takes a professional touch; for the companion at home, all that is required is a good instructor

◆ LEFT
Combing the whiskers and leg hair every day will keep him looking neat.

makes a handy-sized companion for people of all ages, from the busy family to the senior citizen who needs a friend; possibly the best Utility breed from the companion point of view.

◆ ABOVE LEFT
The Miniature Schnauzer is reliable, robust and agile but, above all, adaptable.

◆ BELOW
Black is an officially recognized colour for the Miniature Schnauzer, although there are not many of them.

BREED BOX

Size	small-medium dog: 36 cm (14 in), 9 kg (20 lb) bitch: 33 cm (13 in), 7.5 kg (16½ lb)
Grooming	straightforward
Exercise	medium
Feeding	undemanding
Temperament	alert and intelligent

and a wire-glove. The breed comes in black, black and silver or, most commonly, in what is officially termed "pepper and salt", but to most people would be a dark grey.

What makes the Schnauzer family so distinctive is their ears, which are set up high on their heads and tip forward towards the temple; in addition, they tend to grow luxurious eyebrows and beards.

The Miniature Schnauzer gives the impression of doing everything on the double; he enjoys exercise but does not grumble if he is not out and about all the time. He is not noisy. He

◆ RIGHT
The likeness to a terrier is obvious. Apart from the Schnauzer, the Affenpinscher and the Miniature Pinscher played a part in its development.

POODLES

The Poodle comes in three sizes, Standard, Miniature and Toy, and a number of whole colours. Some countries place the Toy Poodle in the Toy Group. The breed has certain unusual features, chief among which is that the coat is single and does not shed. It is often recommended as a suitable dog for those people who suffer from an allergy to dog hair or dust.

The Poodle's intelligence is renowned; he can be taught all manner of skills, from water-retrieving to circus tricks. He appears to enjoy performing, and the praise and laughter that result.

The Poodle's shape is common to all three heights, with a proud, chiselled face and skull, an elegant neck, and a sound body and legs; the tail is often docked to half its normal length, but this is not compulsory.

◆ LEFT
Poodles are intrinsically neat, whatever their size; this white Standard sits as if perched on a pedestal.

The largest, which is referred to as the Standard Poodle, has a minimum height of 38 cm (15 in); the Miniature between 28 and 38 cm (11–15 in); the Toy should measure less than 28 cm (11 in). Most Standards are considerably taller than the minimum height officially allowed.

The Standard tends to be a real tomboy of a dog, racing about field or park, but returning rapidly if reasonably well trained. The Miniature and Toy sizes are equally happy extroverts but better suited to town

◆ ABOVE
An old breed from Germany, the Standard Poodle was originally a water-retrieving dog.

◆ LEFT
This is the best known show cut, and is meant to protect the dog's chest, kidney and leg joints.

BREED BOX	
Size	three sizes Standard: over 38 cm (15 in), 30–34 kg (66–75 lb) Miniature: 28–38 cm (11–15 in), 6 kg (13 lb) Toy: maximum 28 cm (11 in), 4.5 kg (10 lb)
Grooming	demanding
Exercise	medium
Feeding	straightforward
Temperament	sparky and cheerful

✦ BELOW
Underneath the huge coat is a dog that measures less than 38 cm (15 in) high.

✦ RIGHT
The Miniature Poodle trimmed and groomed for a show. Companion animals do not need to be trimmed like this, although regular attention is still essential.

✦ LEFT AND RIGHT
Apricot is not a common colour for a Toy but is very attractive at its best. Usually it tends to lighten as the dog gets older, but this one is still a rich colour.

✦ BELOW
The Toy Poodle has the same herding, guarding and water-retrieving background as the Standard. These chocolate, black and apricot Toys are very neatly groomed.

life. They can be picked up easily.

The range of colours includes white, cream, apricot, blue, silver, chocolate and black. Grooming is a specialist job. Left untouched the harsh-textured coat will grow to extraordinary lengths. Some form of trimming is essential at regular intervals, and the choice of cut varies from the simple "lamb" to the so-called "lion". Professional demonstration is necessary, even if an owner chooses to learn a do-it-yourself technique.

At one time, the Toys were accused of being finicky feeders, but well-bred specimens are as hardy as either of the larger sizes. The Poodle, whatever the size, is a companion dog *par excellence*.

SCHIPPERKE

The Schipperke hails from Belgium. He is a spitz-type dog of around 36 cm (14 in) in height. His erectly pricked ears and his not over-long neck, combined with a stocky body, give him a compact look. He is usually docked, but if left alone, his tail tends to curl up and over his back in true spitz fashion.

He sports a densely harsh coat, which is black, and less frequently cream or fawn-gold. It is very simple to groom and keep shining with a brush and a rough cloth. He is a brisk mover and delights in exercise over any distance. He is an easy-going character who will eat what he is given. He makes a very good house-dog as he has a sharp bark coupled with sharp hearing.

BREED BOX	
Size	small 22–36 cm (9–14 in), 5.5–7.5 kg (12–16½ lb)
Grooming	easy
Exercise	medium
Feeding	medium
Temperament	intelligent and amiable

◆ ABOVE LEFT
Sometimes known as the Belgian Barge Dog, the Schipperke is both neat and sharp whether lying or . . .

◆ BELOW
. . . standing like the sentry he becomes if told to be on guard.

SCHNAUZER

The Schnauzer (Standard Schnauzer, Working Group) is the middle size of the Schnauzer family. He stands up to 48 cm (19 in) at the withers and is a handsome compact dog who appears fiercer than he actually is. He is in his element as a companion to a busy household, for which he provides a very useful warning signal at the approach of visitors, whether friend or foe, with a loudish, sharp bark.

He has the same short, harsh coat as the Miniature, and it comes in some of the same colours, i.e. pepper and salt as well as black. Grooming is no problem even after a muddy walk. He loves exercise and does not refuse however much is offered, especially if children are included in the equation. He does not run to too much flesh provided his daily intake of food is regulated.

◆ LEFT
Prominent eyebrows and whiskers are the hallmarks of the Schnauzer breeds.

BREED BOX	
Size	medium dog: 48.5 cm (19 in), 18kg (39½ lb) bitch: 45.5 cm (18 in), 16 kg (35 lb)
Grooming	straightforward
Exercise	medium
Feeding	medium
Temperament	alert and reliable

◆ LEFT
The middle-sized Schnauzer is deservedly increasing in popularity. A lively, trustworthy companion, he makes a good house-dog.

SHAR PEI

The Shar Pei, also known as the Chinese Shar-Pei, is a breed of great distinction. He has become well known because of his unusual appearance, with his wrinkly skin and frowning expression.

His head-shape is rectangular with little taper from occiput to nostrils, and his lips and muzzle are well padded. He has inherited a tendency to be born with in-rolling eyelids (entropion), and this can cause

problems. He is born with very wrinkled skin and unfortunately the wrinkles remain into his adult life; skin problems can occur as a result. The earliest exports were not blessed with the most perfect of temperaments.

Those who like the breed obviously appreciate the Shar Pei's unusual appearance, while those who find him ugly will steer clear. He stands up to 51 cm (20 in) tall and is powerfully built, mounted on reasonably firm legs.

In any country where there is a very small pool of breeding stock, faults will multiply. The breed has improved over the past ten or fifteen years, but it would be wise to decide on the selection of such an unusual dog only after long, careful consideration of its qualities and detailed discussions with responsible long-term devotees of the breed.

+ ABOVE
The loose skin and wrinkles are abundant in puppies but may be limited to the head, neck and withers of an older dog.

+ FAR LEFT
The Shar Pei has a large head and a well-padded muzzle.

+ LEFT
The Shar Pei almost became extinct in its native China following the prohibition of dogs. Breeders in Hong Kong kept the Shar Pei line going.

BREED BOX

Size	medium 46–51 cm (18½–20 in), 16–20kg (35–44 lb)
Grooming	medium
Exercise	medium
Feeding	medium
Temperament	independent but friendly

SHIH TZU

The Shih Tzu (Toy Group) originated in China. He has a host of admirers who greatly appreciate his wide-eyed expression and his distinctly cavalier attitude to the world about him. He views that world from a fairly small frame which is only some 26.5 cm (10½ in) high, but he gives the

♦ BELOW
Shih Tzus are sturdy, bouncy extroverts that make delightful family companions.

♦ ABOVE
The golden head typifies a breed that is totally convinced of its superiority.

impression of mental superiority in no uncertain terms.

He has a long, dense coat, which rewards hard work and gets distinctly ragged if neglected. He comes in a

glorious variety of colours, often with a white blaze to his forehead, and he carries his high-set tail like a banner over his back. He definitely enjoys being part of the family, but does not suggest that he is anxious to partake in long, muddy tramps across the fields. He takes a fair deal of cleaning up if he does feel an urge towards outdoor forays in mid-winter.

BREED BOX

Size	small
	dog: 26.5 cm (10½ in)
	bitch: 23 cm (9 in)
	4.5–7.5 kg
	(10–16½ lb)
Grooming	demanding
Exercise	reasonable
Feeding	reasonable
Temperament	friendly and
	independent

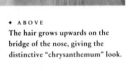

♦ ABOVE
The hair grows upwards on the bridge of the nose, giving the distinctive "chrysanthemum" look.

♦ LEFT
This beautiful coat gives a very good idea of the work involved in grooming a Shih Tzu to show standard.

TIBETAN SPANIEL

The Tibetan Spaniel (Non-Sporting Group) is a neat, tidy dog standing only 25.5 cm (10 in). His coat is longish and silky but does not take as much grooming to keep it looking good as you would at first expect.

He turns up in all sorts of colours, but a golden-red is the most common.

He also comes in a mixture of fawn and white. He has slightly bowed front legs, but this should not be an excuse for him to be grossly unsound.

His nature is accommodating in the household, being happy-go-lucky. He takes naturally to climbing over garden rockeries with gay abandon or rushing around the garden with his family. He does not spend his time looking for food, and he makes a delightful household companion.

+ LEFT
An unfussy breed that does not demand endless grooming.

+ BELOW
The Tibetan Spaniel's original purpose was to act as a companion and watchdog in the monasteries of Tibet.

BREED BOX

Size	small 25.5 cm (10 in), 4–7 kg (9–15½ lb)
Grooming	medium
Exercise	undemanding
Feeding	reasonable
Temperament	Loyal and independent

TIBETAN TERRIER

The Tibetan Terrier (Non-Sporting Group) is a profusely coated, square-built dog, standing as high as 40 cm (16 in). His coat is fine, although with hard brushing it can be made to gleam like silk. He comes in a range of colours from white to black, including golden. He loves people, enjoys plenty of exercise and is extremely nimble and energetic. He eats well, but not greedily. He will act as quite an impressive guard to house and family.

+ ABOVE
A terrier does not usually have such a shiny coat as this, but the Tibetan is, in truth, more of a guard dog.

+ RIGHT
The coat needs regular grooming, which, together with his boundless energy and enthusiasm, means this good-natured dog may be rather overwhelming.

BREED BOX

Size	small-medium 35.5–40 cm (14–16 in), 8–14 kg (18–31 lb)
Grooming	fairly demanding
Exercise	demanding
Feeding	medium
Temperament	outgoing and intelligent

The Working Group

The Working Group has the largest number of breeds and numbers of dogs within breeds. For this reason, in the US and some other countries they have been split into two groups – Working and Herding. These distinctions have been noted in the descriptions of each breed.

The undivided Working Group includes both herding and working, the latter being those breeds that guard, haul and rescue.

The sizes range from the very large Great Dane and the Mastiff, through the middle-sized German Shepherd Dog and the smaller Shetland Sheepdog, to the tiny Lancashire Heeler.

They are mostly extremely predictable dogs, bred for many generations for definite purposes. They have been selected for their trainability and have active minds. Their standard of obedience and their energy go a long way towards accounting for their popularity. Even trained dogs with active minds and bodies can easily become mischievous or difficult to control if they are left too much to their own devices. On the whole they are dogs that need occupation to fill their waking hours.

◆ FACING PAGE **Bullmastiff**

ALASKAN MALAMUTE

The Alaskan Malamute is a big dog; he does not stand as tall as some other giant breeds – 71 cm (28 in) – but he is massively built as befits a dog that is designed to pull heavy weights over snow-covered terrain for vast distances in sub-zero temperatures.

◆ LEFT
The heaviest of the sled dogs, the Alaskan Malamute has a distinctly watchful air.

BREED BOX

Size	giant
	38–56 kg
	(84–123½ lb)
	dog: 64–71 cm
	(25–28 in)
	bitch: 58–66 cm
	(23–26 in)
Grooming	medium
Exercise	demanding
Feeding	demanding
Temperament	reasonably amenable

He can weigh well in excess of 56 kg (123½ lb). Temperamentally he is normally friendly to people, but he can take umbrage with other dogs; a Malamute in full cry after a canine foe is an awesome sight and requires strength and experience in those who have to apply the brakes.

This is a superbly built, handsome breed. His relatively short, harsh, dense coat can be any shade of grey through to black, or from gold through red to liver, with areas of white on his underbelly, mask, legs and feet.

The breed was developed over many generations in Alaska and the Arctic fringes of Canada as a "workhorse", and he uses his ability to pull to great effect when he is on the end of a lead. He needs training from early puppyhood to be controllable in a household situation, so training classes are essential.

He enjoys his food and needs a great deal of exercise from those capable of handling such a giant; he is a delightful dog for those who are ready for a challenge.

◆ RIGHT
The Alaskan Malamute is a powerful, dignified dog. Named after the Mahlemuts, an Innuit tribe, he was used as a draught animal long before Alaska became an American state.

◆ ABOVE
This dog displays a thoroughly handsome and trusting expression, but he is not one to treat in a casual fashion.

ANATOLIAN SHEPHERD DOG

The Anatolian Shepherd Dog comes from Turkey. He is known to his familiars as the Karabash, the Turkish term for his best-known marking, which is cream to fawn in colour and sporting a black mask and ears.

Many European and Asian countries use two distinct types of dog with flocks of sheep. One is for herding and the other for guarding. Shepherd dogs are there to protect flocks against marauding wolves – and marauding humans in the form of rustlers! The Anatolian's height at a top level of 81 cm (32 in) puts him into the range of the awesome; he weighs accordingly. He therefore takes a good deal of feeding.

His coat is short and dense but is not hard to keep tidy. He likes his exercise, but as his ancestors were expected to amble about with the shepherd as the flocks moved from pasture to pasture, he is not often in a hurry.

This breed needs understanding; he will make a good family dog, but the

♦ ABOVE
This is a breed of ancient origin that is regarded as a national emblem in its Turkish homeland.

family must make up its collective mind that his purpose in life is to guard; a few generations of living a softer life has not obliterated the results of careful selection since this mastiff type evolved.

BREED BOX	
Size	giant dog: 74–81 cm (29–32 in), 50–64 kg (110–141 lb) bitch: 71–79 cm (28–31 in), 41–59 kg (90½–130 lb)
Grooming	easy
Exercise	demanding
Feeding	demanding
Temperament	bold and independent

♦ BELOW
A family group, all complete with the prized black mask that gives the breed the popular name of Karabash.

AUSTRALIAN CATTLE DOG

◆ RIGHT AND BELOW LEFT
These dogs are not over-tall, but are very thick-set and possess powerful jaws and surprisingly large teeth.

The Australian Cattle Dog (Herding Group) is a relatively recent immigrant to Britain and North America. He is a true working dog, whose alternative name in his country of origin is the Queensland Heeler.

Heelers persuade cattle to move by taking a quick nip at their heels, a practice not without danger of rapid retaliation! Good cattle-ranching Heelers have selected themselves effectively by their ability to survive the flashing bovine hooves. They are equally agile in the household situation, revelling in all the exercise they can get. They are loyal and biddable.

A robust breed standing a maximum 51 cm (20 in), the Australian Cattle Dog packs a lot of solid muscle into what is a relatively small frame. The official colours of the short, dense coat are blue mottled or red speckled, but they have to be seen to be properly appreciated. They are easy dogs to keep and groom.

BREED BOX

Size	small-medium 16–20 kg (35–44 lb) dog: 46–51 cm (18–20 in) bitch: 43–48 cm (17–19 in)
Grooming	easy
Exercise	medium
Feeding	medium
Temperament	alert and trustworthy

AUSTRALIAN SHEPHERD DOG

The Australian Shepherd Dog (Herding Group) originated in the United States. The Australians claim no credit for him. Exactly how he got his official name is not clear, but the important thing to recognize is that he is a soundly made working dog of considerable charm.

He stands up to 58 cm (23 in) high and has a medium-length coat that is not difficult to groom. He comes in various colours – blue merle, red merle, black or red, all with tan in his head area and on his lower legs.

He is an athletic sort who gives the impression of being capable of working with farm stock most effectively, and who greets friend and stranger openly and without aggression. He needs exercise to keep him fit but will not pester to go out.

◆ ABOVE AND BELOW
This all-purpose dog is capable of herding and guarding; a good performer in obedience and agility competitions.

BREED BOX

Size	medium-large 46–58 cm (18–23 in), 16–32 kg (35–70½ lb)
Grooming	reasonable
Exercise	demanding
Feeding	medium
Temperament	even-tempered

BEARDED COLLIE

The Bearded Collie (Herding Group) possesses bewitching eyes! He can make the toughest heart melt just by standing still and looking soft; hence his enormous increase in popularity over the last three decades. Standing up to 56 cm (22 in) at his withers, he

◆ BELOW
The Bearded Collie has pure Scottish ancestry and retains the basic instincts of a worker.

◆ LEFT
These keen observant eyes are one of the breed's most attractive features.

moves with athletic grace on legs and feet which, like his whole body, are covered with a harsh, shaggy coat underlaid by a soft, close undercoat.

The coat takes plenty of effort to groom as it is capable of picking up a good deal of the countryside in which he greatly prefers to spend his days. Colours range from all shades of grey, through black, blue and sandy, all

with white on head, brisket and lower limbs; he is rounded off with the typical beard after which he takes his name.

The Bearded Collie looks what he is – a cheerful, fun-loving rogue – and has converted well from his original role as a farm worker to make a superb companion and family friend.

BREED BOX	
Size	medium 18–27 kg (39½–59½ lb) dog: 53–56 cm (21–22 in) bitch: 51–53 cm (20–21 in)
Grooming	demanding
Exercise	demanding
Feeding	medium
Temperament	lively, cheerful

◆ BELOW
Quiet while lying waiting, these dogs will move like a flash when the order is given.

BELGIAN SHEPHERD DOG

The Belgian Shepherd Dog (Herding Group) stands as high as 66 cm (26 in) at his tallest, so he is quite sizeable, but he does not carry a great deal of bulky muscle. He is an agile, swift-moving, elegant dog, with a graceful head and neck.

He has been selected over many decades to act as both herder and guard, so he is not instantly friendly to everyone.

There are three distinct coat types and four colour patterns. They originated as variants from different areas of Belgium. The two with long, straight top-coats are the Groenendael,

black (Belgian Sheepdog), and the Tervueren, which is red, fawn or grey, with a black overlay (Belgian Tervueren). The smooth-coated version is the Malinois, which is the same colour as the Tervueren (Belgian Malinois), while a harsh, wiry coat, usually reddish fawn, fits the Laekenois.

An active, working breed, these dogs require plenty of exercise and training. Failure by owners to occupy such intelligent minds can easily lead to the development of mischievous habits. This is a breed for those with the will and the time to enjoy the company of a canine all-rounder.

♦ ABOVE
A wiry-coated Laekenois looks very different from the other varieties of Belgian Shepherd Dog.

BREED BOX

Size	medium–large 56–66 cm (22–26 in), 27.5–28.5 kg (60½–63 lb)
Grooming	medium
Exercise	demanding
Feeding	medium
Temperament	reserved

♦ ABOVE
The Laekenois has hair growing around his eyes, but it should not obscure them.

♦ LEFT
The Groenendael has a long-haired black coat, sometimes with frosting – white or grey hairs – around the muzzle.

♦ LEFT
In Belgium these dogs are classified as separate breeds. In the US the Groenendael is the Belgian Sheepdog, and the Laekenois is not recognized.

◆ BELOW
For many devotees, the most glamorous of all the Belgian Shepherd Dogs is the Tervueren.

◆ LEFT
The Tervueren has a black mask on his face and black ears.

◆ RIGHT
The only smooth-coated Belgian Shepherd Dog is the Malinois.

◆ LEFT
In spite of the difference in coat type and colour, all four dogs are the same basic shape.

BERGAMASCO

The Bergamasco is one of the most recent exports from Italy; like so many others, he has long been used as a herding dog and a guard dog in the mountains, and he has strong protective instincts. It is too early to give much indication of how well he will settle in as a member of a family household.

He stands up to 62 cm (24½ in) high and can weigh as much as 38 kg (84 lb). He is solid and powerful, expects exercise, not necessarily at a great pace, and will eat appropriately for his size.

His most distinctive feature is his coat, which can be solid grey or black with any shade of grey and a certain amount of white; light fawn is also seen. The coat itself is abundant and harsh.

◆ LEFT
The Bergamasco's coat, described as greasy to the touch, makes him appear unkempt, but also keeps him warm and dry. It tends to form loose mats.

BREED BOX	
Size	large 56–62 cm (22–24½ in), 26–38 kg (57½–84 lb)
Grooming	demanding
Exercise	demanding
Feeding	medium
Temperament	cautious, intelligent

◆ BELOW
Grooming may be a problem with this breed.

BERNESE MOUNTAIN DOG

◆ BELOW
The cheerful nature of this ancient breed comes over very clearly as this dog gazes attentively upwards at his owner.

The Bernese Mountain Dog is a handsome, affable fellow. At his tallest he reaches a height of 70 cm (27½ in) and he is built on sturdy lines. His laid-back temperament allied to a great love of his food means he tends to be overweight.

His coat is soft and wavy and responds to vigorous brushing by producing a real sheen. It is basically black with patches of reddish brown, a striking white blaze on the head and a white cross on the chest. He is an intelligent, trainable dog, full of *bonhomie* and courtesy which makes him a very suitable member of a country household. This is not a dog for the town dweller.

He was originally a draught dog and will pull a light cart with evident enjoyment.

◆ RIGHT
The white blaze and cross on the head and chest are characteristic of this handsome Swiss dog.

◆ LEFT
The massiveness of the bone of the leg and the power of the shoulders show why the Bernese is a favourite for pulling dog-carts.

BREED BOX	
Size	large
	40–44 kg (88–97 lb)dog: 64–70 cm (25–27½ in)
	bitch: 58–66 cm (23–26 in)
Grooming	medium
Exercise	medium
Feeding	medium–large
Temperament	good-natured

BORDER COLLIE

The Border Collie (Herding Group) is the classic farm dog. He is neat; he is agile; he thinks on his feet, and if his owner does not occupy his mind with useful training he will get into mischief, because his brain is always active.

Ideally he stands some 53 cm (21 in) at his withers, though he may look lower to ground as he travels at speed in a form of permanent crouch. His eyes show keen

◆ LEFT
The low-slung body of the Border Collie is essential for his super-agile performance at work.

BREED BOX	
Size	small–medium dog: 53 cm (21 in), 23.5 kg (52 lb) bitch: 51 cm (20 in), 19 kg (42 lb)
Grooming	medium
Exercise	demanding
Feeding	medium
Temperament	very alert and trainable

To put it bluntly, he does not suffer fools gladly, and he is not averse to taking a swift nip at those who do not get his point, in the same way that he will liven the reactions of the sheep or cattle which are his natural flock.

◆ LEFT
This is the sharp expression of what is, by common consent, the most trainable breed of them all.

◆ BELOW
Working dogs from the Scottish borders, this is a breed that needs to be constantly occupied if destructive behaviour is to be avoided.

intelligence and his type is the favourite for those who wish to compete at top level in obedience competitions.

His coat is usually moderately long but is relatively easy to groom as long as the tangles are dealt with on a regular basis. He comes in all kinds of colours with white, but the commonest base colour is black. He demands exercise for his muscles just as much as for his brain. He makes an ideal family dog for the grown family, but he is not best suited to be a nursemaid to the very young, though no doubt such heresy will raise a few protests.

BOUVIER DES FLANDRES

The Bouvier des Flandres (Herding Group) is a powerful and rugged-looking dog. His basic role in life is herding both cattle and sheep, but over the years he has adapted to town life to a surprising degree. He has found favour with police forces not only in his native Belgium, but in Britain and several other countries.

He stands up to 68 cm (27½ in) and weighs solidly to match; he sports a coat which is coarse both to touch and to view. He also carries a beard and moustache, which add to his fairly fearsome appearance; coupled with a colour that ranges from fawn through brindle to black, he might be thought forbidding,but, in fact, he is a trustworthy character and fully deserves his increasing popularity as a house-companion for those who enjoy a strong dog.

BREED BOX	
Size	large dog: 62–68 cm (24½–27½ in), 35–40 kg (77–88 lb) bitch: 59–65 cm (23½–25½ in), 27–35 kg (60–77 lb)
Grooming	fairly demanding
Exercise	medium
Feeding	medium
Temperament	calm and sensible

♦ ABOVE
Bouvier des Flandres are solid and stable dogs. That, combined with their size and forbidding expression, has encouraged several police forces to train them for service.

♦ BELOW
Despite his expression the Bouvier des Flandres is an aimiable dog unless provoked.

♦ RIGHT
The Bouvier was once a cattle dog in is native Belgium and was also used to pull carts. He is balanced in body and limb, a true power-pack.

♦ ABOVE
The ears are small and high set.

BOXER

The Boxer is one of the canine world's characters! He is rightly recognized by his vast army of devotees as an extrovert. He is intelligent but needs to be convinced that his owner knows best – any other relationship is liable to be a disaster.

He stands up to 63 cm (25 in) high, and his supple limbs and body are well covered with muscle. He is full of stamina; he considers that his family household are his to guard, and woe betide anyone who does not recognize the fact.

His coat is simple to keep clean and neat; his colour ranges from red-fawn through various shades of brindle, with degrees of white. Some Boxers are born entirely white; a percentage of these are deaf from birth and as a result, many breeders put them down.

He is not a particularly greedy dog, but his appetite needs control if he is not to become overweight. His concept of exercise is that life is to be lived at speed. He can be trained to be obedient, but those who set out to

◆ LEFT
Originating in Germany, the Boxer's ancestors were used for hunting wild boar and deer. Today he has one of the most distinctive shapes of all dogs.

BREED BOX	
Size	medium dog: 57–63 cm (22½–25 in), 30–32 kg (66–70½ lb) bitch: 57–59 cm (21–23½ in), 25–27 kg (55–59½ lb)
Grooming	easy
Exercise	demanding
Feeding	medium
Temperament	biddable and fearless

harness this canine power-pack need to realize what they are facing.

His pugnacious upturned chin gives him the appearance of a pugilist; he does not start fights frequently, but he never backs down if challenged.

◆ ABOVE
Nothing gets past those flashing eyes. The Boxer is one of the best guarding breeds.

◆ RIGHT
A rare sight – a relaxed Boxer – but he will still react in a flash if he needs to.

BRIARD

The Briard (Herding Group) is from
France. He has a Gallic charm about
him which captivates a good number
of folk. He has a rugged appearance,
subtly combined with a slightly dapper
look. At up to 68 cm (27 in) tall, he is
a big dog, but underneath the long,
wavy coat he is not a heavyweight.

The coat comes in black, slate grey
or varying shades of fawn. It needs
regular grooming, especially as the
breed thoroughly enjoys exercise in
town or country and can bring the
great outdoors back indoors on
returning home. The Briard is one of a
mere handful of breeds that not only

◆ LEFT
This is a breed which takes up a fair
amount of space and needs a considerable
degree of effort to keep tidy.

◆ BELOW
In spite of all the
hair they carry round
their eyes, Briards
are extremely sharp-
eyed.

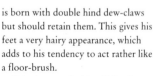

BREED BOX

Size	large
	dog: 62–68 cm
	(24½–27 in),
	38.5 kg (85 lb)
	bitch: 56–64 cm
	(22–25 in), 34 kg
	(75 lb)
Grooming	demanding
Exercise	demanding
Feeding	demanding
Temperament	lively and intelligent

is born with double hind dew-claws
but should retain them. This gives his
feet a very hairy appearance, which
adds to his tendency to act rather like
a floor-brush.

Briards are trainable; all that is
needed is determination and patience.
The dog must have total confidence in
his owner. When he plays, he plays
rough. He is good with children, but
perhaps not with toddlers; they may
get knocked over. This, of course, is
true of many breeds, but it would be
wise to remember that this handsome
dog started off as a guarding dog for
flocks of nomadic sheep.

◆ LEFT
The Briard is a very impressive animal
with a kindly disposition, but capable of
being a very effective guard.

BULLMASTIFF

The Bullmastiff evolved from crossing the Old English Mastiff with the Bulldog, to produce a very effective guard dog. In an age in which several large guarding breeds have been imported into Britain from mainland Europe, the original role of the Bullmastiff as a gamekeeper's assistant has tended to be forgotten.

He stands as much as 69 cm (27 in) high and weighs up to 59 kg (130 lb), which means he is both big and powerful. He is not to be trifled with; he does not suffer fools gladly, so he merits ownership by those who appreciate his cardinal virtue, utter faithfulness, and can handle a dog of independent nature.

He has a close fitting, hard coat, which can be brindle, fawn or red. He does not take a great deal of effort to keep clean and neat. He is muscular all over. His head is reminiscent of the old-fashioned Bulldog of the nineteenth century, which had a longer nose than in modern times. He does not therefore suffer the breathing problems that beset some brachycephalic breeds and enjoys exercise without being over-demanding.

◆ BELOW
This original gamekeeper's dog can achieve a truly awesome turn of speed in spite of his size.

◆ LEFT
The power of the jaw is obvious.

◆ BELOW LEFT
As befits a reliable guard dog, the Bullmastiff is noted for his alertness.

◆ BELOW RIGHT
This is an extremely strong dog that may be stubborn and over-protective; not one for the novice owner.

BREED BOX

Size	large to giant dog: 63.5–69 cm (25–27 in), 50–59 kg (110–130 lb) bitch: 61–66 cm (24–26 in), 41–50 kg (90–110 lb)
Grooming	easy
Exercise	medium
Feeding	demanding
Temperament	reserved, faithful

ROUGH COLLIE

The Rough Collie (Collie, Herding Group), from Scotland, has a dignified and intelligent expression. The Rough Collie stands up to 61 cm (24 in) high. He has three basic coat colours: cream to gold sable, tricolour and blue merle, which is a clear silver-blue splashed

◆ LEFT
This is the breed known to the world as the "Lassie" dog of film fame.

◆ BELOW
This Rough Collie shows why the breed is known for its most attractive expression.

BREED BOX	
Size	medium–large dog: 56–61 cm (22–24½ in), 20.5–29.5 kg (45–65 lb)
Grooming	demanding
Exercise	medium
Feeding	medium
Temperament	friendly

with black. All three include white to some degree. The breed has a considerable history as working sheepdogs, but has not been used in this fashion to any great extent for a long time. Consequently the old, fast-moving Collie is not so obvious, and the dogs we see today tend to be a trifle idle. They do, however, make wonderful pets and household companions.

SMOOTH COLLIE

The Smooth Collie (Collie, Herding Group), also from Scotland, is simply the Rough Collie without the long coat. His coat is short and flat. He comes in the same colour variations as the Rough, although blue merles are more obvious in the Smooth.

The Smooth Collie is, if anything, more active than the Rough, and he expects more exercise. He makes an excellent household member but has never achieved the popularity levels of the "Lassie" dog, maybe because his short coat lacks film-star glamour.

◆ ABOVE RIGHT
The Smooth has moderately large ears, carried semi-erect when alert.

◆ LEFT
The Smooth version of the better known Rough Collie revealing the shape the coat hides.

BREED BOX	
Size	medium–large measurements as the Rough Collie
Grooming	simple
Exercise	medium
Feeding	medium
Temperament	gay and friendly

DOBERMANN

♦ LEFT
Well controlled, the Dobermann is as good
a guard dog as any.

The Dobermann (still known in the US as the Doberman Pinscher) originates from Germany and is a tough, fast-moving guard dog. He was bred selectively by Herr Louis Dobermann as an all-purpose tracking/police dog. He is built on clean, powerful lines and reaches ideally 69 cm (27 in) at the withers.

His short, close-lying coat responds to polishing with a true gleam. He is most commonly seen as black, with tan colouring on the muzzle, forechest, legs and feet; but the black can be replaced by red or blue, or even, more rarely, with fawn.

He is energy personified, and at one time had a reputation for being bad-tempered. Careful, sensible selection and training has altered this to a very large extent, but he is still a dog that needs to know who is going to be the boss in any family or work-place. As a house-dog, he ranks with any breed for faithful performance. He demands exercise as a right and needs a sizeable amount of food as a result.

♦ RIGHT
A soft expression is the result of leaving
the ears uncropped, as in the UK.

♦ RIGHT
This elegant and powerful breed has an
enormous following throughout the world
but frightens some people.

BREED BOX

Size	large
	dog: 69 cm (27½ in), 37.5 kg (83 lb)
	bitch: 65 cm (25½ in), 33 kg (73 lb)
Grooming	simple
Exercise	demanding
Feeding	medium–demanding
Temperament	alert and biddable

ESKIMO DOG

♦ LEFT
The Eskimo Dog
follows very much in
the tradition of the
polar exploration
dogs, willing to lie
for hours waiting for
the next task.

The Eskimo Dog (American Eskimo Dog) is one of a group of husky types. He is smaller than the Alaskan Malamute, but thicker set than the Siberian Husky. He was bred to haul fairly weighty sleighs over snow for the Inuit people ; temperament was not important. He is the classic dog portrayed in books on polar exploration; he had to fight for his very existence.

It is important to recognize such facts, as this dog stands 68 cm (27 in) high and weighs up to 47 kg (104 lb). When he decides to pull on lead or harness he does just that, he pulls. He has a thick double coat of any known dog colour, and grooming him is hard work.

He eats well and voraciously. Training him takes time and patience.

♦ ABOVE
These dogs display a watchful eye and a somewhat reserved attitude to people.

♦ LEFT
The coat protects against the rawest of cold weather – essential for the hard-working role for which he was bred.

BREED BOX	
Size	medium–large dog: 58–68 cm (23–27 in), 34–47 kg (75–104 lb) bitch: 51–61 cm (20–24 in), 27–41 kg (59½–90½ lb)
Grooming	demanding
Exercise	demanding
Feeding	demanding
Temperament	wary and alert

ESTRELA MOUNTAIN DOG

The Estrela Mountain Dog is a sturdy, sizeable dog of the mastiff type, which comes from the mountainous regions of Portugal.

This is a well-mannered breed with a delightfully shambling way of going. He regards people as friends and enjoys living with a family. He also enjoys exercise as befits his size, at a top level of 72 cm (28½ in) at his withers. He eats well but is not greedy.

His coat is usually fairly long and comes in fawn, brindle or wolf grey, but the general impression is of a large benign dog with a dark muzzle. Grooming him is not a huge problem. He has a loud bark and will give a good account of himself if his household is threatened, but he is not a difficult dog to handle, being relatively amenable to training.

◆ ABOVE
The Estrela Mountain Dog looks what he is – massive and kindly.

BREED BOX

Size	large–medium
	30–50 kg
	(66–110 lb)
	dog: 65–72 cm
	(25½–28½ in)
	bitch: 62–68 cm
	(24½–27½ in)
Grooming	medium
Exercise	medium
Feeding	medium
Temperament	loyal but stubborn

◆ ABOVE
The benign expression of eye is the key to the personality.

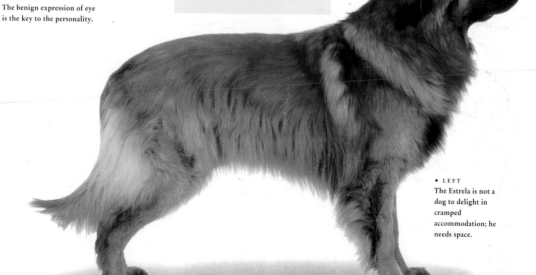

◆ LEFT
The Estrela is not a dog to delight in cramped accommodation; he needs space.

FINNISH LAPPHUND

The Finnish Lapphund is yet another spitz type from the Nordic countries. Standing an average 47 cm (18½ in), he is a handsome dog with a bright expression, wide-set prick ears, and a tail carried over the back.

A solidly made dog, his profuse, coarse outer coat requires regular grooming. The coat colours may be any of a variety all over, but shades other than the main tone are seen on the head, chest and tail-tip, giving him a striking and attractive appearance.

He could make a useful companion/watchdog for any household as he is sensible and of good stature. He is rare outside his native country of Finland.

BREED BOX

Size	medium–small 46–52 cm (18–20½ in), 20–21 kg (44–46 lb)
Grooming	fairly demanding
Exercise	medium
Feeding	medium
Temperament	calm and intelligent

 TOP
The Finnish Lapphund is a typical spitz-type, originally used to herd reindeer.

 ABOVE
This sharp, intense look befits his character exactly.

 LEFT
The breed is not often seen outside Finland but is a sensible size for a small family home.

GERMAN SHEPHERD DOG (ALSATIAN)

The German Shepherd Dog (Herding Group) must be the best known breed of them all. His breeding and training have led to his renown as a herding sheepdog, a leader of the blind and as a police dog. Police forces, the armed services, prison officers, drug officers and private protection agencies all over the world employ the GSD.

There are considerable variations in what is regarded as the ideal shape for this multi-purpose dog. Traditionally, the dog is a proud, powerful creature, standing an average 63 cm (25 in), with a body length slightly greater than its height. Coat lengths vary; some enthusiasts state that a medium length coat is the only acceptable version, while others accept a long-haired type. Colours include black, black and tan, and sable. White and cream dogs do occur, but raise loud, horrified protests from many aficionados, something to bear in mind if the ultimate intention is to show the dog. All such matters of taste aside, the fact remains that, at his best, the GSD is an intelligent, trainable dog with a pleasant, loyal disposition and makes a first-class household member. He needs exercise and, on occasion, may need to be stimulated in that direction as he can be wilfully idle. On the other hand, most need to have their energies directed into useful pursuits as the GSD, in common with so many breeds in the Working Group, originated as a shepherd dog.

+ TOP RIGHT
The eyes show the breed's intelligence – the GSD does not miss a trick.

+ RIGHT
A handsome all-purpose dog that enjoys walking.

BREED BOX

Size	large
	dog: 60–66 cm
	(24–26 in), 36.5 kg
	(80½ lb)
	bitch: 55–60 cm
	(22–24 in),
	29.5 kg (65 lb)
Grooming	medium
Exercise	demanding
Feeding	medium
Temperament	steady, highly
	trainable

GIANT SCHNAUZER

The Giant Schnauzer is the largest of the three Schnauzer varieties. This big dog is very similar in shape to his smaller cousins, being a clean-cut, square-built dog that can stand as high as 70 cm (27½ in) at his withers. He is found in the same colours – black or pepper and salt – as the smaller ones, but naturally he is a more imposing looking animal.

At one time employed as a cattle-droving dog, he has become popular as a household guard dog in Germany and Britain. He also has a role as a

police dog in Europe because he is highly trainable and loyal.

He needs regular trimming, he enjoys family life, he does not eat a vast amount considering his size, and his beard and moustache give him the sort of expression that will impress those with felonious intent.

+ LEFT
The Giant Schnauzer has a distinctively moulded head and huge eyebrows.

+ ABOVE
This is a no-nonsense breed used in Europe for police work. It is not aggressive unless provoked.

+ RIGHT
In some countries the Giant Schnauzer's ears are cropped.

BREED BOX	
Size	large dog: 65–70 cm (25½–27½ in), 45.5 kg (100 lb) bitch: 60–65 cm (23½–25½ in), 41 kg (90 lb)
Grooming	medium
Exercise	medium
Feeding	medium
Temperament	bold and good- natured

+ LEFT
The Giant Schnauzer will keenly defend his territory. It is not a breed to be treated casually.

GREAT DANE

The Great Dane is a true giant among dogs; he stands an absolute minimum of 76 cm (30 in), but the adult male should be considerably taller. His coat is short and dense, and therefore relatively easy to keep neat and sleek.

He has five official colours, which are jealously guarded by the breed enthusiasts – brindle, fawn, blue, black and harlequin, the latter being a basic white with all black or all blue patches that give the appearance of being torn at the edges. Any other colour is a freak, and it is unwise to pay extra money on the suggestion that "this unusual colour is very rare and therefore is more valuable".

BREED BOX

Size	giant
	dog: minimum
	76 cm (30 in),
	54 kg (119 lb)
	bitch: minimum
	71 cm (28 in),
	46 kg (101½ lb)
Grooming	simple
Exercise	medium
Feeding	demanding
Temperament	kindly but dignified

He is a strong, deep-chested dog but is truly a hound used for chasing wild boar in his native country, which is Germany, not Denmark. He can be trained to be reasonably obedient

♦ ABOVE RIGHT
The Dane is remarkably gentle for such a huge creature.

because he is intelligent. He likes both exercise and his creature comforts; he recognizes the pleasure of occupying the major part of the hearth in front of a roaring fire. For those who see him as the dog of all dogs and can afford his large appetite, he is a must; but, like all giant dogs, he has a regrettable tendency to have a shortish life span.

♦ RIGHT
This brindle bitch takes up a lot of space – she won't curl up easily in a small house.

♦ ABOVE
The Dane's head is big, carried high, giving the impression of strength.

HOVAWART

The Hovawart (pronounced "hoffavart") is a guard dog from the Black Forest region of Bavaria. He wears a medium length coat, which can be black and gold, a goldish blond or, on occasion, black by itself. He stands up to 70 cm (27½ in), but he is not a heavy-bodied dog.

He has yet to make his mark outside of Bavaria, but he is trainable, enjoys family life, and does not demand vast amounts of exercise or food. He is possessed of a good nose, so he will follow a scent, which suggests that he could become a canine all-rounder.

BREED BOX

Size	medium–large dog: 63–70cm (25–27½ in), 30–40 kg (66–88 lb) bitch: 58–65 cm (23–25½ in), 25–35 kg (55–77 lb)
Grooming	medium
Exercise	medium
Feeding	medium
Temperament	alert, intelligent, wilful

✦ ABOVE RIGHT
The black and gold colour gleams on this fit, athletic native of the Black Forest.

✦ RIGHT
A friendly look in a breed that enjoys human company.

✦ BELOW
The Kuvasz comes from a cold climate, hence his thick coat.

HUNGARIAN KUVASZ

The Hungarian Kuvasz (Kuvasz) has quite a presence in the United States. He is of the style seen in many European countries acting, as a guard or herder; he is cautious of strangers.

A prospective owner requires considerable experience of handling difficult dogs before introducing the Hungarian Kuvasz into normal household circumstances.

He stands up to 75 cm (29½ in) tall, wears a medium-length, thick coat, which is pure white and reasonably groomable. He requires a fair amount of exercise, is of burly build and eats accordingly.

✦ LEFT
This brilliant white dog never relaxes his guard. He is thought to have found his way to Hungary with nomadic Turkish shepherds sometime during the Middle Ages.

BREED BOX

Size	large 66–75 cm (26–29½ in), 30–52 kg (66–115 lb)
Grooming	medium
Exercise	medium
Feeding	demanding
Temperament	trainable, wary

HUNGARIAN PULI

The Hungarian Puli (Puli, Herding Group) is a herding dog, and typifies the cliché "once seen, never forgotten". His coat varies from black, through grey and fawn to apricot. It grows massively into a weather-resistant equivalent of the Eskimo's parka. It will withstand cold and wet. As the dog matures the coat tends to form into cords.

These cords are not to be confused with the mats that are the sign of an idle owner. The coat takes a great amount of hard work to keep in order. The cords cover the dog literally from head to toe and include the face and tail. There is, indeed, very little visible of the dog beneath the coat. When the dog moves the cords swing *en masse*

♦ RIGHT
A mid-European dog with a highly distinctive corded coat which swings like a loose rug as he goes on his energetic way.

rather like a curtain. The Hungarian Puli is a fast-moving energetic creature who loves exercise and people. He is a great barker and therefore an effective burglar alarm. This is a dog for the devotee.

BREED BOX	
Size	small
	dog: 40–44 cm
	(16–17½ in), 13–
	15 kg (28½–33 lb)
	bitch: 37–41 cm
	(14½–16½ in),
	10–13 kg
	(22–28½ lb)
Grooming	very demanding
Exercise	medium
Feeding	undemanding
Temperament	lively but reserved with strangers

KOMONDOR

♦ RIGHT
In spite of the coat over his eyes, the Komondor misses nothing.

The Komondor is another dog from Hungary, where he guards flocks and farms. He has a huge, corded coat that reaches the ground in the adult. It is white immediately after the dog has been bathed and dried; drying him is a long drawn-out process. His whiteness tends to be rapidly compromised by contact with the countryside. His average height is 80 cm (31½ in), and he weighs about 50 kg (110 lb), so he is an awesome chap once roused.

His ancestry is as a farm dog; bringing such a dog into a town atmosphere is totally misguided. His basic instinct is to guard, and to trifle with a dog of such dimensions is risky, to put it mildly. This is definitely a dog only for those who understand what they are taking on.

♦ RIGHT
This is a dog for the wide open spaces and those with time to maintain him.

BREED BOX	
Size	giant
	dog: minimum 65 cm (25½ in), 50–
	51 kg (110–112½ lb)
	bitch: minimum 60 cm (23½ in), 36–
	50 kg (79½–110 lb)
Grooming	very demanding
Exercise	medium
Feeding	medium
Temperament	wary, protective

121

LANCASHIRE HEELER

The Lancashire Heeler is a stylish little dog. He stands a mere 30 cm (12 in) high and is slightly longer than he is tall. His forelegs tend to be slightly bowed, but this should not be excessive. As his name implies, he was used on farms to herd cattle and he still does when required.

His coat is not truly short, but it does not grow to any great length. He is always black and tan and a thorough, brisk grooming will have him shining in no time at all. He enjoys exercise, but he does not make an issue of it. He makes a terrific household companion and appears to love children and joining in games.

He has a sharp bark which is louder than one might expect from such a small package, he eats well and is highly biddable.

♦ LEFT
A small and active dog that adapts easily from droving to being part of a household. The original Lancashire Heelers were used to drive cattle by nipping at their heels, much like the Welsh Corgi.

BREED BOX

Size	small
	6.5 kg (14 lb) dog:
	30 cm (12 in)
	bitch: 25 cm (10 in)
Grooming	easy
Exercise	medium
Feeding	undemanding
Temperament	happy and affectionate

♦ ABOVE
The prick ears betoken the dog's readiness to join in any form of fun.

♦ LEFT
Short legs carry a powerful little body; this breed will clear the house of rats just as a bonus.

MAREMMA SHEEPDOG

The Maremma Sheepdog is Italy's version of the nomadic flock-guarder. As such this is a dog that has derived from generations of working guard dogs. He stands as high as 73 cm (29 in), but he is not heavily built.

He has been seen in Britain, but not the US, for some twenty years in

◆ LEFT AND BELOW FAR LEFT
This dog's ancestry means that he requires plenty of exercise as well as discipline.

steadily increasing numbers, and his temperament has gradually altered from the initial sharpness which was to be expected from this type of import. Now he is a fairly trainable dog of good basic intelligence, even if still a trifle aloof with strangers.

He carries a medium-length coat that fits him closely; it is white with a slight touch of fawn. He has an alert expression that denotes the watchfulness of his ancestry. He is a worker and requires exercise to keep him the fit, muscular creature that his breeding has made him.

◆ BELOW
An expression that suggests that he is not a fawning dog; he will take his time to admit strangers to the bosom of his family.

BREED BOX

Size	large
	dog: 65–73 cm (25½–29 in), 35–45 kg (77–99 lb)
	bitch: 60–68 cm (24–27½ in), 30–40 kg (66–88 lb)
Grooming	medium
Exercise	demanding
Feeding	medium
Temperament	lively, active

MASTIFF

The Mastiff is often referred to as the Old English Mastiff. He stands up to 76 cm (30 in) and is built on massive lines. Giant dogs such as this grow remarkably quickly and require care in feeding; they do eat a lot and can be expensive to rear. In addition a dog

✦ RIGHT
The hindlegs are not always well formed, so care has to be taken in selecting a sound puppy.

✦ BELOW LEFT
The breed is usually good-natured but nevertheless has massive jaws in a very solid head.

BREED BOX	
Size	giant 70–76 cm (27½–30 in), 79–86 kg (174–189½ lb)
Grooming	simple
Exercise	medium
Feeding	demanding
Temperament	steady

that weighs as much as many an owner requires determination as well as ability to control it. Although the Mastiff is not demanding as regards exercise, he still needs an adequate amount of freedom.

This dog has a short-lying coat that is reasonably easy to keep in order. The colour varies from apricot-fawn to a dark brindle-fawn, always combined with a black mask and ears.

Fortunately he has a calm temperament – if not he would be dangerous.

NEAPOLITAN MASTIFF

The Neapolitan Mastiff has the usual mastiff square-shaped head and muzzle, powerful body, and strong limbs. In addition he sports a quantity of loose skin around jowls

and dewlap, coupled with pendulous lips, which give his head a huge appearance.

His short, dense coat is tight fitting on body and limbs; it is usually black or blue-grey, but occasionally brown shades are seen. He enjoys exercise but is not over-demanding in this respect; he does boast a fairly large appetite. He is undoubtedly courageous and protective of owner and property. His devotees state that he will only use his full force on command, which comes as a relief to those who do not own him.

Grooming him is not a great problem, although, like so many breeds that have loose jowls, he dribbles, and when he shakes his head he may prove a trifle anti-social.

✦ ABOVE
The Neapolitan Mastiff may be descended from the war and fighting dogs of Ancient Rome.

✦ LEFT
The skin folds down the neck are there to protect vital structures from attack.

BREED BOX	
Size	giant 65–75 cm (25½–29 in), 50–70 kg (110–154 lb)
Grooming	undemanding
Exercise	medium
Feeding	fairly demanding
Temperament	devoted guard

NEWFOUNDLAND

◆ BELOW
The Newfoundland has immense charm
and a sense of humour.

The Newfoundland is a massive cuddly bear of a dog. His large face radiates *bonhomie*. He is a water-dog *par excellence* to the extent that his fanciers warn purchasers that if they do not want to be forcibly rescued from water, they should not go swimming with a Newfoundland! He is known to everyone as "The Newfie".

He can stand up to 71 cm (28 in) high, not all that tall by some standards, but his body is built on generous lines as are his legs, which end in feet with webs between his toes to help him swim strongly at speed. He weighs up to 69 kg (152 lb) and eats to match.

He has an all-embracing coat which has a slightly oily feel to it. Not

BREED BOX	
Size	giant
	dog: 71 cm (28 in),
	64–69 kg (141–
	152 lb)
	bitch: 66 cm (26 in),
	50–54.5 kg
	(110–120 lb)
Grooming	fairly demanding
Exercise	aquatically
	demanding
Feeding	demanding
Temperament	delightfully docile

surprisingly, this renders it totally waterproof. The colour can be black, brown, or white with black markings, which is generally known as Landseer (because Sir Edwin Landseer included Newfoundlands of this marking in many of his paintings).

In spite of being an aquatic dog, he has his own style of movement on *terra firma* – he tends to roll in a charming, nautical fashion. He expects exercise, but prefers it to be in water; then, when he gets back home, he has an engaging habit of shaking vigorously. This is a dog for the whole family, but not for the house-proud or the flat-dweller.

◆ ABOVE
The rather deep-set eyes give an expression of benign relaxation.

◆ ABOVE
A house needs plenty of room to accommodate a Newfie.

◆ LEFT
The lung space is evident even in a front view of this master-swimmer among dogs.

NORWEGIAN BUHUND

The Norwegian Buhund is a neatly shaped spitz. He has erect ears on an intelligent head and a lively attitude to life. He measures around 45 cm (18 in), so he is not at all an imposing dog, but he has an air of alertness about him that makes people pay attention.

BREED BOX

Size	medium–small 41–46 cm (16–18 in), 24–26 kg (53–57 lb)
Grooming	undemanding
Exercise	medium
Feeding	undemanding
Temperament	energetic and fearless

✦ RIGHT
This is the archetypal outline of a spitz; all neatness and expectancy. He was once used as a sled-dog in his native country.

✦ RIGHT
The Norwegian Buhund is an easy dog to keep clean; he gives the impression of disliking getting very muddy.

His coat is close and harsh; the commonest colour is a wheaten gold, but dogs with black and wolf-sable coats are seen. The coat is short enough to require no great skill or time to keep groomed.

He is a herder in his native Norway, and good hearing allows him to react swiftly as a guard. He gets on well with his family but is somewhat reserved with those he does not know. He thoroughly enjoys exercise and is relatively biddable, so his bustling style can be kept under control when loose in field or park.

✦ LEFT
This is a breed of energetic dogs that may be initially wary of strangers but fits family life well.

OLD ENGLISH SHEEPDOG

The Old English Sheepdog (Herding Group), nicknamed the Bobtail, is another of those breeds that could be classified as distinctive the world over. He has evolved from a practical, working-style sheepdog into a stylized show-dog; his use in commercial advertising has led to a growth in popularity, sadly to the breed's overall detriment.

He stands around 61 cm (24 in) high, but his huge, fluffed-up coat makes him look somewhat taller. The owners who exhibit their dogs have to put in hours of work in order to maintain them in show-ring style. Left ungroomed for any length of time, the harsh-textured coat can become

◆ LEFT
Old English Sheepdogs are known as Bobtails because their tails are customarily docked.

◆ BELOW LEFT
This breed goes back at least 150 years, possibly longer.

◆ BELOW RIGHT
The higher rump end is the result of grooming the hair upwards.

matted to a degree that leaves little alternative but to clip.

He is a cheerful extrovert and makes a good family companion, provided the family is committed to the dog's exercise and can cope with

his occasionally explosive nature. He will join in every possible activity with enthusiasm. He is capable of being a first-class guard of his owner's property, with a highly distinctive bark to emphasize his presence.

BREED BOX	
Size	large dog: minimum 61 cm (24 in), 36.5 kg (80½ lb) bitch: minimum 56 cm (22 in), 29.5 kg (65 lb)
Grooming	very demanding
Exercise	medium
Feeding	medium
Temperament	friendly and outgoing

PINSCHER

The Pinscher, originally from Germany, is best described as a midway stage between the Dobermann and the tiny Miniature Pinscher. He wears the same short, dense coat in the same basic black-and-tan colour combination of the Dobermann, with the same alternatives of red, blue and fawn with tan.

He is a sharp-outlined dog, with an alert-looking head and expression, and a neat, muscled body. He moves with nimble athletic strides. As he stands

BREED BOX	
Size	medium–small
	43–48 cm (17–19 in)
Grooming	easy
Exercise	medium
Feeding	undemanding
Temperament	active and confident

◆ LEFT
The Pinscher is a very bright breed with clean-cut features and bright eyes.

◆ ABOVE
This red-coat version positively shines to prove the dog's health.

up to 48 cm (19 in), he is capable of accepting plenty of exercise and can make a splendid member of either a town or country family.

He needs minimal grooming to polish him into a glossy shine; he does not ask for excessive food, and he possesses a sharp voice and an intelligent mind, which makes him a handy watchdog.

◆ LEFT
Although he can be distrustful of strangers, the Pinscher is responsive to training and makes a good family member.

◆ LEFT
A charming sheepdog from Poland with a friendly attitude, which has brought him great popularity.

POLISH LOWLAND SHEEPDOG

The Polish Lowland Sheepdog is thought to be descended from the ancient Asian herding dogs. It nearly became extinct during World War II, but since then careful breeding has ensured its survival. Standing around 52 cm (20½ in), he has a cheerful look about his well-haired face, and he is a truly active working herder.

He has been often compared to a smaller version of the Bearded Collie; both breeds are also extremely intelligent and trainable. He is good-natured to the extent that he makes a thoroughly balanced family companion and children's playmate.

He needs plenty of exercise and can be boisterous; his coat is long and harsh, with a density to his soft undercoat that guarantees he will find cold winters no problem after his native Poland. Grooming has to be thorough, but the breed is very tolerant.

◆ BELOW
The Polish Lowland Sheepdog is usually born without a tail. His long thick coat needs regular grooming.

BREED BOX

Size	medium–small dog: 43–52 cm (17–20½ in), 19.5 kg (43 lb) bitch: 40–46 cm (16–18 in)
Grooming	demanding
Exercise	demanding
Feeding	medium
Temperament	alert, biddable

PORTUGUESE WATER DOG

The Portuguese Water Dog is commonly mistaken for the Standard Poodle; he stands up to 57 cm (22½ in), has a profuse coat, and is brown or black in basic coloration. He has not got the refined head of the Poodle, but he does have a traditional trim, clipped from behind the rib-cage.

His tail is not docked but is clipped except for a sizeable plume at the end. This trim is based on his role as a swimmer; he has been taught by Portuguese fishermen to retrieve lost nets. These dogs have exaggerated webs on their feet to help them to swim.

He is reputed to be stubborn, so he requires firm handling. He adores freedom of exercise, and he makes a good family dog with a cheerful attitude.

◆ LEFT
These dogs are similar to the Poodle but without such a refined head.

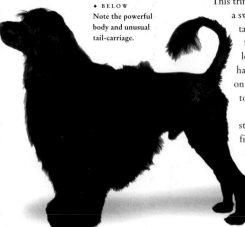

◆ BELOW
Note the powerful body and unusual tail-carriage.

BREED BOX

Size	medium–large dog: 50–57 cm (20–22½ in), 19–25 kg (42–55 lb) bitch: 43–52 cm (17–20½ in), 16–22 kg (35–48½ lb)
Grooming	demanding
Exercise	demanding
Feeding	medium
Temperament	tireless and amenable

PYRENEAN MOUNTAIN DOG

The Pyrenean Mountain Dog, also known as the Great Pyrenees, is a solidly built animal measuring as much as 70 cm (27½ in) and weighing up to 60 kg (132 lb). He is another of the

LEFT
The Pyrenean Mountain Dog is massive and requires a firm handler. A steady-moving dog with very considerable dignity, he can be quite reserved with strangers.

BREED BOX

Size	giant
	dog: 70 cm (27½ in), 50-60 kg (119-132 lb)
	bitch: minimum 65 cm (25½ in), 40 kg (88 lb)
Grooming	demanding
Exercise	medium
Feeding	demanding
Temperament	confident and genial

flock-guarding dogs of the European nomad shepherd; with his coarse-textured white coat he merges into the flock. As a domestic house-dog he requires regular grooming; bathing him is no easy task.

The modern Pyrenean has more of the permitted badger coloration, especially on head and ears, than twenty or thirty years ago. He is another breed that grows large double hind dewclaws, which help him in snow-covered terrain.

He does not require excessive exercise and normally moves at a dignified amble in park or pasture. He makes a good household member, his basic temperament having become more gentle as a result of generations of selective breeding worldwide.

PYRENEAN SHEEPDOG

The Pyrenean Sheepdog is a very recent introduction to Britain and is not registered in the US. He stands up to 48 cm (19 in) high and appears neat in general outline with a lean body. His coat is

fairly harsh with a somewhat windswept look; it is supported by a thickish undercoat. Colour can vary from fawn through grey to merle and black or black and white.

He is a smallish dog for an all-purpose flock-guarder, but he gives an impression of speed and enjoys exercise. It is too early to predict his suitability as a general family dog.

◆ LEFT AND ABOVE
This second breed from the Pyrenees is totally different in looks. Both breeds work with sheep but perform in contrasting styles.

BREED BOX

Size	medium–small 38–48 cm (15–19 in), 8–15 kg (18–33 lb)
Grooming	medium
Exercise	medium
Feeding	undemanding
Temperament	alert, wary

ROTTWEILER

The Rottweiler, from Germany, is a handsome and striking breed. The males can stand as tall as 69 cm (27 in), and they are solidly built of hard muscle.

Unfortunately their popularity has not done the breed good service as the ease of selling any standard of Rottweiler proved too attractive for

unscrupulous dealers. It was predictable that such a powerful dog would be all too capable of inflicting great damage if he attacked humans, and in the late 1980s this happened. The numbers of Rottweilers being bred dropped dramatically, and this dangerous situation levelled off. The

breed is very intelligent, but there is a considerable difference in temperament between the dog and the bitch, the latter in general being calmer and her reactions easier to predict.

BREED BOX

Size	large
	dog: 63–69 cm
	(25–27½ in),
	50 kg (110 lb)
	bitch: 58–63.5 cm
	(23–25 in),
	38.5 kg (85 lb)
Grooming	simple
Exercise	medium-demanding
Feeding	demanding
Temperament	courageous,
	trainable

The coat is invariably of medium-short length and black and tan in colour. Grooming is rewarding; it produces a magnificent shine very easily. Exercise is essential because of the muscular nature of the breed. He likes his food and expects plenty.

This is a breed for experienced dog owners who will devote time and attention to the dog. He merits much of the enthusiasm he engenders but needs good control.

+ ABOVE
The powerful muzzle shows why the breed has earned respect as a guard.

+ TOP RIGHT
An average-sized, strong, agile dog, the Rottweiler is not for the nervous owner or for newcomers to dogs.

+ LEFT
The Rottweiler will respect the authority of an owner who merits it – handler and dog need training.

ST BERNARD

The St Bernard is yet another instantly recognizable breed. He stands tall, but it is his massive frame that makes him so remarkable. He originated in the mountains of Switzerland and is traditionally depicted with a miniature brandy-barrel attached to his collar as

◆ RIGHT
These dogs were first taken to the famous Hospice in the Swiss Alps by the monks as guards and companions in the seventeenth century.

BREED BOX

Size	giant
	maximum 91.5 cm
	(36 in)
	dog: 75 kg
	(165½ lb)
	bitch: 68 kg (150 lb)
Grooming	medium-demanding
Exercise	medium
Feeding	demanding
Temperament	steady and
	benevolent

he locates the traveller stranded in deep snow.

Everything about the modern St Bernard is huge, right down to his feet. He has a great breadth of skull and huge jaws. His lower lip tends to droop at the outside corner, which means that he drools a fair amount.

His limbs are big-boned, so rearing the young is expensive and needs to be well understood. Exercise in the puppy should be increased very slowly as he grows to ensure that the minimum strain is put on tender tissues. Exercise in the adult is usually a gentle progression, though a St Bernard pulling on his lead can be a struggle for the handler. Grooming is

not a problem except that there is a lot of coat to be dealt with. The coat is normally medium length, but there is a short-coated St Bernard. The colour can be orange, red brindle or

◆ ABOVE RIGHT
It is all too easy to fall for the delightful charm of the youngster.

◆ LEFT
St Bernards are massive dogs with truly powerful bones in the forelegs.

mahogany brindle with white markings, or white with any of the above as coloured patches.

Temperamentally the breed is trustworthy and benign, which is just as well, since the rare occasion when a St Bernard does erupt is awesome to view. This is an attractive breed, but those who fall for him should consider carefully how well they can cope.

SAMOYED

The Samoyed is the "Laughing Cavalier" of dogdom, with his brilliant white colour and his typical spitz expression. He stands up to 56 cm (22 in) high, and he is very slightly longer than tall. His coat is harsh and stand-off, in a basic white, but many of the breed carry varying amounts of

◆ LEFT
This is a happy-go-lucky breed with never a nasty thought, though plenty of mischievous ones.

biscuit, which is a light reddish fawn.
Grooming is hard work, but Samoyeds are tolerant and will submit for hours, if necessary, to lying on their sides while the owners brush and comb them. The breed has a history as a sled-dog and has hairy, flat feet to enable it to cope with ice that would otherwise pack into the spaces between the pads.

He enjoys exercise, but needs human company; he is a super member of a family household, but still manages to be a great companion to those who live alone. He is not a huge eater, in spite of his energetic lifestyle. His only real drawback is his tendency to bark noisily, especially when he is enjoying himself, which is most of the time.

◆ FAR LEFT
Samoyeds have a smiling and cheerful expression.

◆ BELOW
Under the coat, there is usually a muscular frame that fits well into a sled-harness, given the opportunity. The breed originated with the Samoyeds, a nomadic tribe of northern Asia.

BREED BOX

Size	medium-large dog: 51–56 cm (20–22 in), 23 kg (50½ lb) bitch: 46–51 cm (18–20 in), 18 kg (39½ lb)
Grooming	very demanding
Exercise	medium
Feeding	medium
Temperament	alert and smiling

SHETLAND SHEEPDOG

The Shetland Sheepdog (Herding Group) is a diminutive version of the Rough Collie, although few companion dogs are genuinely as small as the official top height permitted for show dogs, which is around 37 cm (14½ in). In fact, this very attractive little dog has all the instincts that his name implies and, although today he is very much a family dog, he is still capable of reacting as a worker.

◆ RIGHT
The slight tilt of the head, as if asking a question, is typical of the Sheltie.

◆ BELOW RIGHT
This miniature version of the Rough Collie is a worker in its own right.

BREED BOX

Size	small
	9 kg (20 lb)
	dog: 37 cm (14½ in)
	bitch: 35.5 cm
	(14 in)
Grooming	demanding
Exercise	medium
Feeding	undemanding
Temperament	affectionate and responsive

He carries a long, straight top-coat that can be coloured sable, tricolour, blue merle, black and white, and even black and tan. The undercoat is thick, so it requires thorough grooming fairly frequently if it is not to become matted and impossible to cope with.

He is an alert dog and will take a great deal of exercise if it is offered but can just as easily make a first-class companion for an elderly person. He is watchful and capable of giving tongue when the occasion demands it.

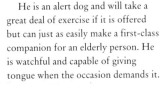

◆ BELOW
Shelties are sturdy, cheerful and easy to train. They are also photogenic!

SIBERIAN HUSKY

The Siberian Husky is the racer of the sled-dog world. It may seem a hard thing to say about what, in many ways, is a very charming dog indeed, but he lives only to pull a sledge! He stands up to 60 cm (23½ in) at the withers, he

is lean at his muscular best, and he has a head that is distinctly reminiscent of a wolf, but with a kinder look.

His coat is fairly long and will keep him warm in the most bitter cold. He can come in virtually any colour or pattern of colours. His eyes are the most remarkable feature of his face as they too can vary in colour, even to the extent of one being brown and the other blue. If that was not odd

enough, dogs are found whose individual irises can show two halves of different hues.

His attitude to people is of extreme tolerance; to his own kind he can be very domineering, and there is a distinct pecking order in a racing pack. It is possible to persuade the odd one to walk on a loose lead and even obey basic commands, but it simply is not his idea of how a dog should behave. People who keep them usually exercise them in front of a sledge if snow is available or by pulling a wheeled rig on forest tracks. Husky racing events take place all over Britain, America and Europe. Think carefully before choosing him as a companion animal.

✦ ABOVE
These dogs can jump a good height from a standstill.

BREED BOX	
Size	medium-large dog: 60 cm (23½ in) 23.5 kg (52 lb) bitch: 53.5 cm (21 in), 19.5 kg (43 lb)
Grooming	medium
Exercise	very demanding
Feeding	demanding
Temperament	friendly but reserved

✦ ABOVE
The Siberian Husky rarely lowers his pricked ears.

✦ RIGHT
Originally draught dogs with the Inuit people, half a dozen Siberian Huskies attached to a racing sledge will give an exciting ride.

✦ LEFT
Note the strength of the legs, which keep racing Huskies on the move.

135

SWEDISH LAPPHUND

The Swedish Lapphund is built on very similar lines to the Finnish Lapphund. He may stand up to 51 cm (20 in) and is of typical spitz construction. His coat is weather resistant and of medium length; it is a mixture of black and brown with an

✦ RIGHT
This stout-framed dog has a coat fir to withstand Scandinavian weather.

✦ BELOW
The Swedish Lapphund has a relatively gentle character.

BREED BOX	
Size	medium-small
	44–51 cm (20 in),
	19.5–20.5 kg
	(43–45 lb)
Grooming	medium
Exercise	medium
Feeding	medium
Temperament	active and friendly

occasional touch of white on his chest or feet. He is not difficult to groom.

He appears to be a friendly, intelligent dog. His temperament would appeal to a family household as he enjoys exercise and is not greedy. He is not, as yet, well known outside his native country.

SWEDISH VALLHUND

The Swedish Vallhund looks and acts very much like a grey or yellowish Corgi. He is built on similar lines, standing a mere 35 cm (14 in) tall, but somewhat longer in body than height.

His job is to herd and he does this, as do the Corgis, by nipping at the heels of cattle that are not as quick to move as required.

He is cheerful with sharply erect ears and is steadily gaining in popularity, although not registered in the US. He makes an excellent family companion as he delights in exercise and human friendship.

His coat is reasonably short, harsh and easy to keep in shape. He comes in grey, greyish brown and varying shades of yellow with reddish brown thrown in.

✦ ABOVE
If you're looking for real intelligence in a dog's expression, it is to be found in this charmer.

BREED BOX	
Size	small
	dog: 33–35 cm
	(13–14 in)
	bitch: 31–33 cm
	(12½–13 in)
	11.5–13 kg
	(25½–28½ lb)
Grooming	undemanding
Exercise	medium
Feeding	undemanding
Temperament	friendly and eager

✦ RIGHT
The Swedish Vallhund is a low-to-ground, heeler type, agile, nimble and very biddable.

TIBETAN MASTIFF

The Tibetan Mastiff is an unusual member of the mastiff world because he has a longish coat. He has a genial expression, but odd specimens can be touchy. On the whole they are likeable creatures with coats of varying colours, ranging from black, through black and tan, to gold and grey.

He stands up to 66 cm (26 in), which means he is not a giant, but his body is solidly made. He is also unusual for a mastiff in that he carries his tail high and over his back. He is a useful guard dog and enjoys his exercise, but those who choose him should be ready to handle a powerful dog.

◆ ABOVE
A genial eye may belie a distrustful temperament – not a dog for the casual.

◆ ABOVE
Well suited to his native Tibet, he needs thorough grooming if he is destined to live indoors.

◆ RIGHT
Most European mastiffs are descended from this breed, which was saved from extinction last century.

BREED BOX

Size	large
	66 cm (26 in)
	64–82 kg
	(141–181 lb)
Grooming	fairly demanding
Exercise	medium
Feeding	demanding
Temperament	aloof and protective

WELSH CORGI (CARDIGAN)

The Welsh Corgi (Herding Group) comes in two separate versions: the Cardigan and the Pembroke. The Cardigan Corgi stands ideally 30 cm (12 in) at the withers; he is relatively long-cast on sturdy, short legs. He is unlike his Pembroke cousin in that he carries a full tail, which is long and very well coated. He is not hard work to groom, nor is he greedy.

Colour-wise he can be almost any dog colour, though white should not predominate. He has large, erect ears and an intelligent eye. He does not bustle about very rapidly and is

◆ LEFT
Cardigan Corgis come in a range of colour schemes and have large ears set well back.

prepared to take life as it comes, though when working with cattle he has to be nimble enough to nip a heel and avoid the retaliatory kick.

As a member of a household he has a curiously benign attitude, but can raise the alarm vociferously if his territory is invaded.

◆ BELOW FAR LEFT
A watchful expression is typical of this ancient breed.

◆ ABOVE
Blue eyes only occur in blue merle dogs.

BREED BOX

Size	small
	30 cm (12 in)
	dog: 11 kg (24 lb)
	bitch: 10 kg (22 lb)
Grooming	medium
Exercise	medium
Feeding	undemanding
Temperament	alert and steady

◆ LEFT
The Cardigan is solidly built on short sturdy legs.

WELSH CORGI (PEMBROKE)

The Pembroke (Herding Group) is
the better known version of the Corgi.
He customarily sports a docked tail.
He stands 30.5 cm (12 in) at the
withers and has a longish body. He is
sturdily built with a sharp, bright
expression and prick ears.

He has a straight dense coat of
medium length and is not difficult to

♦ LEFT
The better known
Corgi – the
Pembroke – usually
comes in red and
white.

BREED BOX

Size	small
	25.5–30.5 cm
	(10–12 in)
	dog: 10–12 kg
	(22–26½ lb)
	bitch: 10–11 kg
	(22–24 lb)
Grooming	medium
Exercise	medium
Feeding	medium
Temperament	workmanlike and
	active

groom once he has dried off after a
country walk. The most common
colour is red with white markings, but
he does come in sable, fawn or even
black and tan.

He is traditionally a cattle-drover,
hence his occasional tendency to nip
the heels of humans rather than cattle.
His slightly doubtful temperament of
previous times seems to have
improved over the last decade.

He is a popular household dog with
families who enjoy his brisk, energetic
attitude to life, but he has a slight
tendency to over-eat so he needs
rationing on occasion.

♦ ABOVE
This is a practical and adaptable breed, friendly
and full of stamina.

♦ BELOW
This young dog displays all the charm of a breed
whose purpose is to walk cattle, even if he isn't
very big.

♦ ABOVE
His foxy head should show an intelligent and
alert expression.

The Toy Group

The Toy Group is made up of breeds that are among the smallest of all.
The largest are the ever-popular Cavalier King Charles Spaniel, the Chinese
Crested Dog and the Lowchen, while at the other end of the scale are the
Pomeranian and the Chihuahua. Height measurements are not given in many of
the Kennel Club's official Breed Standards; rather, these tend to give ideal
weights or weight ranges.

The name Toy is in some ways misleading; admittedly some of the breeds
tend to appear to be animated playthings, but their temperaments suggest that
they are anything but. The breeds included have some common factors, such as
the ability to be picked up and carried easily, but they vary widely in size, type
and behaviour. The misconception to avoid is that they are all dear little things
who behave impeccably and do not take any effort to look after.

♦ FACING PAGE Yorkshire Terrier

AFFENPINSCHER

The Affenpinscher, originally from Germany, is a dog that makes people laugh. He is said to resemble a monkey facially, and certainly his twinkling eyes give his expression a thoroughly mischievous glint. He stands up to 28 cm (11 in) high and weighs 3–4 kg (6½–9lb).

He has a coat that is harsh in texture and generally looks pretty untidy, so grooming him is not an over-serious business. He is game for fun and is capable of taking part in family activities as his muzzle is not so exaggeratedly short as to interfere with his breathing to any real extent.

He is normally black all over, although a grey coloration does sometimes appear. As a house companion, he is one of the best because he is fearless and delights in confronting any intruder.

◆ LEFT
A sense of mischief prevails whenever two or more Affenpinschers are gathered together.

◆ BELOW
The tail is often left undocked and curls gently over the back when the dog is moving.

BREED BOX

Size	small
	24–28 cm
	(9½–11 in),
	3–4 kg (6½–9 lb)
Grooming	medium
Exercise	medium
Feeding	undemanding
Temperament	lively and self-confident

◆ BELOW
The coat is rough and of uneven length over the body – shaggy in some places, shorter in others. This is a truly hairy specimen.

◆ ABOVE
The greying effect produces a remarkable facial study.

AUSTRALIAN SILKY TERRIER

The Australian Silky Terrier, known variously as the Sidney Silky or just the Silky, is a mixture produced from cross-breeding the Australian Terrier and the Yorkshire Terrier. The result is a sharp-featured, silky-coated dog that stands some 23 cm (9 in) high at the withers.

One would expect any animal produced by mating one from Australia with one from Yorkshire to

♦ LEFT
A compact dog, Silkies may have been bred primarily as household companions, but they are also pretty good rat-catchers.

♦ BELOW LEFT
At times Silkies can put on quite a serious expression, not accurate evidence of their true temperament.

♦ RIGHT
Silkies should have small, cat-like feet and no long hair on the legs.

BREED BOX

Size	small
	23 cm (9in),
	4 kg (9 lb)
Grooming	medium
Exercise	medium
Feeding	undemanding
Temperament	alert and friendly

be only too capable of holding his own, so the term "silky" should never mislead anyone into thinking it denotes anything soft. Not a bit of it – he is full of character!

His coat, which is fairly long and straight, comes in blue and tan or greyish blue and tan, and with minimal brushing can become glossy. He is intended as a household companion and does the job splendidly.

♦ RIGHT
In silhouette the essential sharpness of outline and the fixed gaze become obvious – a good mixture of toy and terrier.

BICHON FRISE

The Bichon Frise (Non-Sporting Group) originated in the Mediterranean area and is dazzlingly white in colour. He is as sure of his own importance as any dog could be.

He stands up to 28 cm (11 in) high and is slightly longer in the back than

◆ LEFT
A modern glamour star – with a coat trimmed like topiary; very stylish but hard work to maintain.

BREED BOX

Size	small
	23–28 cm (9–11 in),
	3–6 kg (6½–13 lb)
Grooming	demanding
Exercise	medium
Feeding	medium
Temperament	a friendly extrovert

he is tall. He carries his tail curled high over his back, and his natural coat should be fine and silky with soft corkscrew curls. The canine topiarists have got hold of him, and the corkscrew curls are not seen in the show-ring today. There is no necessity to have his curls scissored off – it costs money and is not obligatory! But he still needs grooming.

He is spritely and enjoys family games; he is another Toy who can cope most adequately with the rush of life's rich pattern in a busy household.

BOLOGNESE

The Bolognese, who has recently started to spread from his native Italy, is a small white dog with a square compact build. He has a distinctive white coat, which is described as flocked and covers the whole dog, head and all.

◆ RIGHT
The Bolognese is a fairly similar dog in type, but with a coat that is not cosseted except to keep it clean and tidy.

BREED BOX

Size	small
	25–31 cm
	(10–12 in),
	3–4 kg (6½–9 lb)
Grooming	fairly demanding
Exercise	medium
Feeding	undemanding
Temperament	happy, alert,
initially	

He stands up to 31 cm (12 in) and, as he is expected to be exhibited in the natural state, he tends to give the impression of a rough-and-ready character, which is unusual in a Toy breed. He does not have an exaggerated trim especially for the show-ring.

His body and legs are well muscled, and he gives the impression of enjoying plenty of free exercise. He comes from the same root stock as the Bichon Frise so is an intelligent dog. He also has the same large, round eyes with black rims.

Those looking for a pleasant, small dog, who is not too tiny, might well consider having a look at the cheerful Bolognese as a household companion.

CAVALIER KING CHARLES SPANIEL

◆ LEFT
A neat breed, ideal for anyone who wants an active and cheerful companion.

The Cavalier King Charles Spaniel (the Cavalier) is a popular Toy dog with everyone. Built on the lines of a small gundog, he has a charm for the elderly as well as the young family. He seems to love people and he does not find fault with other dogs.

His weight range is 5.5–8 kg (12–18 lb), which is a wide enough range, but as a breed they do tend to get even heavier. The Cavalier's placid nature and friendliness often induces people to give him injudicious titbits that encourage obesity!

He has a good-looking head and a well-balanced body. He can appear in a series of colours, from ruby (red), black and tan, and tricolour (black and white with tan markings) to Blenheim, which is a mix of rich chestnut and white, often with a lozenge of chestnut in the centre of a white patch down the middle of his head.

He enjoys exercise and is built on elegant, athletic lines; indeed, he needs it in view of his hearty appetite. He is not difficult to groom as his coat can be kept tidy with normal brush-and-comb techniques; a true favourite.

◆ BELOW
The charm of the Cavalier's expression is beautifully caught in this head-study.

BREED BOX	
Size	small 32 cm (13 in), 5.5–8 kg (12–18 lb)
Grooming	medium
Exercise	medium
Feeding	medium
Temperament	very friendly

◆ BELOW
The Cavalier is in fact a miniature spaniel, combining all the qualities of a Toy and a Gundog.

CHIHUAHUA

◆ LEFT
Three of a kind with
two Smooths and a
Long. This is an alert
breed with a loud
bark that can sound
rather like a duck
quacking.

The Chihuahua probably originated in
South America and indeed is named
after a Mexican state. He comes in two
versions, one of which is smooth-
coated, the other long-coated. Apart
from their coat, they are identical, tiny
dogs of tremendous spirit. They weigh
up to 3 kg (6½ lb), but lighter
specimens are generally preferred in
the show-ring. The Smooth Coat has a
soft, glossy covering of a coat, while
the Long Coat is never coarse and is
relatively easy to keep neat. The
Chihuahua is very proud of his tail,
which he carries high like a flag. It
typifies the breed's personality.

All colours are accepted, but fawn
to red with white is the most
frequently seen.

They are brave dogs, putting up
with pain remarkably stoically, but not
accepting cheek or insult from dogs
vastly larger than themselves. They do
not appreciate humans who invade
their homes without permission,
yelling defiance and threatening
mayhem as they race to defend their
home and family.

Rearing a young Chihuahua puppy
requires care in moving about; a high-
stepping human can very easily
trample on such a tiny creature, so
Chihuahua breeders soon learn to use
a shuffling method of walking. The
breed, however, is not a weak or
delicate one; in fact, the opposite is
true. Both versions enjoy exercise and
are extremely game, but families with
young children must supervise the
interaction between puppy and child
carefully and constantly.

BREED BOX	
Size	very small
	15–23 cm (6–9 in),
	1–3 kg (2–6½ lb)
Grooming	medium
Exercise	undemanding
Feeding	undemanding
Temperament	spirited and
	intelligent

◆ ABOVE
The large, round, bright eyes set wide apart are
a hallmark of a spritely breed.

◆ LEFT
The Chihuahua is a well-proportioned little dog
ready to take on anything.

CHINESE CRESTED DOG

The Chinese Crested Dog comes in two versions, one is largely devoid of hair, the other covered with a veil of long soft hair. The hair colour in both cases is white to silvery white.

BREED BOX

Size	small
	dog: 28–33 cm
	(11–13 in)
	bitch: 23–30 cm
	(9–12 in)
	maximum 5.5 kg
	(12 lb)
Grooming	unusual
Exercise	medium
Feeding	medium
Temperament	cheerful and friendly

◆ LEFT
The Chinese Crested Powder-Puff, at one time seen as an outcast by breeders, now recognized as essential to the future of a very unusual breed.

The Powder Puff is heavier in build than the racy-looking Hairless. Grooming of either type is not demanding; the Hairless dogs feel the cold, although their skin is thick, smooth and tough, and they need extra attention in cold weather. The Chinese Crested dogs are hardy, friendly and affectionate creatures, who are also intelligent and perform well as watchdogs in a family household.

◆ RIGHT
The Hairless version has a crest on the head and neck, a plume on the end of the tail and thick hair on the feet and lower legs.

ENGLISH TOY TERRIER

The English Toy Terrier comes in only one colour pattern, and that is the traditional combination of black and tan. His coat is short, dense and responds with a good gloss to a brisk polishing with a cloth. This neat dog stands an ideal height of 30 cm (12 in) and weighs around the 3 kg (6½ lb) mark, so he is well named.

He has dark, sparkling eyes, and his prominent ears are described by the cognoscenti as candle-flame in shape. To watch him move is a joy if he is sound, because he goes extremely smoothly and easily like a much larger dog in style.

He is friendly and affectionate by nature, and he makes a thoroughly charming companion, with a touch of the terrier in him.

◆ LEFT AND ABOVE RIGHT
Yet another remarkable tiny dog, he makes up for his lack of size by possessing a mighty yap.

BREED BOX

Size	small
	25–30 cm
	(10–12 in),
	2.7–3.5 kg (6–8 lb)
Grooming	simple
Exercise	undemanding
Feeding	undemanding
Temperament	alert and terrier-like

GRIFFON
BRUXELLOIS

✦ LEFT
These dogs sport a walrus
moustache.

The Griffon Bruxellois (Brussels Griffon) from Belgium is one of the characters of the Toy Group. He is truly bright and cheerful. With a monkey-like expression and his usual harsh coat of red, he has the equivalent of canine cheek. There is a smooth-coated version, which is equally pert, and both can come in other colours.

✦ BELOW
Two of a kind, both harsh
in coat, with the less
common black colour in
front.

BREED BOX

Size	small
	18–20 cm (7–8 in),
	2.2–4.9 kg (5–11 lb)
Grooming	medium
Exercise	undemanding
Feeding	undemanding
Temperament	lively and alert

family, but he also makes a cheerful and fearless companion for those who live on their own. He does not take much grooming, but professional stripping on occasion in the rough-coated form is not a bad idea.

He weighs anything from 2.2–4.9 kg (5–11 lb), but the middle of that range is the most usual. He has a bit of the terrier about him, so he thoroughly enjoys his exercise with a boisterous

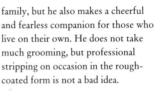

✦ ABOVE
A typical smooth-coated head
with a bright observant eye.

✦ RIGHT AND LEFT
The smooth-coated type
has a solid body on neat
legs and is not too
difficult to keep clean
and tidy.

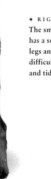

ITALIAN GREYHOUND

♦ LEFT
A miniature Greyhound with nicely balanced musculature in the hindquarters.

The Italian Greyhound, at his best, is a true miniature of the classic Greyhound. He is graceful and nimble in his movements. He weighs 2.7–4.5 kg (6–10 lb), so there is not much of him. Breeders have to steer a fine line between producing a slightly coarse animal or an all too delicate one.

His coat is short and glossy, and his skin is fine; he does not take too kindly to cold weather and will wrap himself up in a blanket quite deliberately. Grooming only requires a piece of silk rubbed over him daily to keep him shining rather like a porcelain model. The colours seen are black, blue, cream, fawn, red and white or any of those broken with white areas. He holds his ears in a quizzical fashion when really interested.

His bones are fine and therefore fairly easy to break. His muscles can be quite impressive, but, in truth, too many dogs appear spindly. This is an elegant, ancient breed, but those who fancy owning one should study them carefully before rushing out to buy the first one offered. He is not suited to life in an energetic family household, until children are old enough to understand the problems of his lightweight stature.

BREED BOX	
Size	small 25.5 cm (10 in), 2.7–4.5 kg (6–10 lb)
Grooming	easy
Exercise	undemanding
Feeding	undemanding
Temperament	intelligent and vivacious

JAPANESE CHIN

The Japanese Chin is a pretty dog by any standards. He has a round shaped head with large eyes that show the white in the inner corners, giving him a permanent look of surprise. His coat is profuse, long and silky, and comes only in black and white or red and white. The ideal weight is 1.8–3.2 kg (4–7 lb), so he is a true Toy, but confident with it.

He gives the impression of having a slightly superior air, but also of being delighted to meet people. In spite of its length, his coat is not difficult to control as long as grooming is regular and thorough. He enjoys a scurry round the garden or a walk round the local park, but is not enthusiastic about long country hikes. More a dog for a quiet existence than a family companion; not suitable for young children.

BREED BOX	
Size	very small maximum 18 cm (7 in), 1.8–3.2 kg (4–7 lb)
Grooming	undemanding
Exercise	undemanding
Feeding	undemanding
Temperament	cheerful and good-natured

♦ RIGHT
The Chin is easily mistaken for the better-known Pekingese but has less prominent eyes, which tend to show white in the inner corners.

KING CHARLES SPANIEL

The King Charles Spaniel is also known as the English Toy Spaniel. He is similar to the Cavalier but has a shorter nose and a more domed head. He has a long, silky coat, which comes in the same colour range as the Cavalier – black and tan, ruby, Blenheim and tricolour – and is equally rewarding to groom.

He is more reserved than the Cavalier but has the same kindly and intelligent disposition. He weighs between 3.6 and 6.3 kg (8–14 lb). He makes a genuine, devoted companion but does not need too much exercise or food.

♦ LEFT
Easily mistaken for the better-known Cavalier King Charles Spaniel, but with a slightly more snubbed nose. The Cavalier was developed from this breed.

♦ BELOW
Another breed that is no longer docked, the tail in its natural state is well feathered and not carried high.

♦ ABOVE
The large dark eyes and long well-feathered ears give him an appealing look.

BREED BOX

Size	small
	3.6–6.3 kg (8–14 lb)
	dog: 25.5 cm (10 in)
	bitch: 20.5 cm (8 in)
Grooming	medium
Exercise	undemanding
Feeding	medium
Temperament	gentle and affectionate

LOWCHEN

The Lowchen or Little Lion Dog is an interesting dog, which originated in Europe. He stands up to 33 cm (13 in) at the withers, so he is not one of the tiny Toys.

He carries a long silky coat of any colour, which forms a mane, and he derives his alternative name from the fact that he is trimmed to resemble a lion; the coat of the body is clipped from behind the last rib and the whole length of the tail except for a plume on the end. Grooming is obviously a real job, but he does not need anything out of the ordinary to keep him neat.

He is active and playful. He gets on very well with children so makes a satisfactory household pet.

+ ABOVE LEFT
A somewhat grave expression belies the fact that the dog can be a real live wire.

+ BELOW
The Lowchen needs clipping to maintain the leonine hind-end and the trimmed tail.

BREED BOX

Size	small
	25–33 cm (10–
	13 in), 3 kg (6½ lb)
Grooming	fairly demanding
Exercise	medium
Feeding	medium
Temperament	intelligent and affectionate

MALTESE

The Maltese (previously known as the Maltese Terrier) is an extremely stylish little dog. He stands up to 25 cm (10 in) tall. His round eye-rims are black and act as a contrast to the whiteness of his long, silky coat – white all over, though occasional lemon markings appear. Grooming such a coat to achieve constant effect is time-consuming, but the results are very rewarding.

He is one of the neatest movers in the Toy Group; at full trot he seems to sail along with his coat billowing around him. He obviously loves exercise and appears to derive enormous pleasure and humour from human company. Any suspicion that he is delicate is totally misplaced; he is surprisingly hardy and spirited. His trusty, lively nature is endearing.

+ LEFT
The all-white coat and the round dark eyes is something breeders have striven to maintain for many centuries, but they have not made a softie of the dog in the process.

BREED BOX

Size	small
	(10 in), 2–3 kg
	(4½–6½ lb)
Grooming	very demanding
Exercise	undemanding
Feeding	undemanding
Temperament	very good-natured

MINIATURE PINSCHER

The Miniature Pinscher (or Min Pin) is the smallest version of the pinscher breeds. He stands up to 30 cm (12 in) high at his withers and wears a hard, short coat that is easily groomed to shine. He comes in black, blue or chocolate with tan, and also various solid shades of red.

He carries his neat ears either pricked or half-dropped on a stylish head. He is sturdy in body and definite in his way of going, which is like that of a Hackney pony. He gives the impression that he loves being loose in a garden or park; he has quick reactions and makes a useful household watchdog.

✦ RIGHT
The large erect ears are very striking in this red-coloured dog, which has his tail undocked.

BREED BOX

Size	small 25.5–30 cm (10–12 in), 3.5 kg (7½ lb)
Grooming	easy
Exercise	medium
Feeding	undemanding
Temperament	alert and courageous

✦ BELOW
The front view shows the neat, straight legs – a toy in stature, athletic in style.

✦ LEFT
This dog has the customary docked tail.

✦ ABOVE
The black and tan coat is the one most often seen.

PAPILLON

The Papillon, or Butterfly Dog, is very attractive. He stands up to 28 cm (11 in) tall on neat, trim legs, and, underneath an easily brushed long, silky coat, he has a surprisingly strong body.

The coat is a basic white with patches of a variety of colours except liver. The traditional markings on his

+ LEFT
The white line down the forehead is said to represent the body of a butterfly, from which the Papillon derives his name.

+ BELOW FAR LEFT
The tall, fringed ears represent the butterfly's wings.

+ BELOW
The whole dog is neatly covered with long, silky hair, but beneath all the glamour is a highly intelligent and trainable animal.

head and large erect ears, with a neat white stripe down the centre of his skull and on to his nose, produce a combined effect resembling the body and open wings of a butterfly, which is how he was given his name.

He can be trained to a high level of obedience and delights in exercise with a household but is not suited to live with very young children in case he gets trodden on.

BREED BOX	
Size	small
	20–28 cm (8–11 in),
	2–2.5 kg (4½–5½ lb)
Grooming	medium
Exercise	medium
Feeding	undemanding
Temperament	lively and most
	intelligent

PEKINGESE

◆ BELOW
Modern Pekes tend to have huge coats; no
matter what a dog looks like, it must be able to
walk freely.

The Pekingese has his roots in ancient China. Tradition tells us that he derives from the palaces of the Tang Dynasty, and this seems to be firmly engrained in his character, although he shows glimpses of a humorous nature on occasion. With a huge personality inside a relatively small body, he is a dog for the devotee.

He has an ideal weight of around 5 kg (11 lb), with the bitches tending to be heavier than the dogs. Inside an apparently small framework are heavily boned legs.

◆ ABOVE
Modern Pekes also have very pretty heads and this picture shows the true beauty of the Peke's expression with lustrous, soft eyes.

He has a broad head and a very short muzzle, which can lead to severe breathing problems; careful selection is necessary to breed healthy Pekes, and there are no short cuts to getting it right.

Exercise is a matter over which Pekes are not ecstatic. They tend to move with a dignified and leisurely roll; consequently country walks are out. The coat, which can be of virtually any hue except albino and liver, is long and profuse. It needs regular and dedicated attention to achieve a creditable result.

BREED BOX	
Size	small
	18 cm (7 in)
	dog: maximum
	5 kg (11 lb)
	bitch: maximum
	5.5 kg (12 lb)
Grooming	demanding
Exercise	undemanding
Feeding	demanding
Temperament	loyal and aloof

◆ BELOW
Pekes were at one time carried by ladies of the Chinese court and referred to as "sleeve dogs".

POMERANIAN

The Pomeranian is the smallest of the five sizes of German Spitz. He weighs up to a mere 2 kg (4½ lb), with the bitches being slightly heavier. His abundant stand-off coat is normally a whole colour such as orange, black or cream through to white. Regular grooming is necessary to achieve the overall look of a ball of fluff.

The margin between the sturdiness, which even this tiny breed should possess, and a shell-like delicateness is a fine one, and some breeders find it

difficult to achieve. Poms exhibit a tremendous amount of energy, pirouetting gaily on the ends of their leads. They are capable of producing a barrage of fairly shrill yapping, which may deter burglars – and interrupt conversation!

◆ LEFT
The Pomeranian at his best is a dog to charm the hardest heart; this tiny character has all the courage of a lion in his eyes.

◆ LEFT
Pomeranians should have an expression of intelligence and complete confidence.

◆ BELOW
A family trio in the best of coats; but do not buy a Pom until you have tried grooming one yourself.

BREED BOX	
Size	very small
	22–28 cm
	(8½–11 in)
	1.8–2 kg (4–4½ lb)
Grooming	demanding
Exercise	undemanding
Feeding	undemanding
Temperament	intelligent and
	extrovert

PUG

The Pug is robust. He weighs up to 8 kg (17½ lb) and is packed tightly into a sturdy, compact frame. He wears a short and smoothly glossy coat, which comes most commonly in fawn but can appear in apricot, silver or black. He traditionally has a black mask. He is easily kept tidy.

He carries his tail tightly curled into a roll on the top of his back, and when he is in his most perky state of

◆ LEFT
An ancient breed of miniaturized mastiffs, Pugs were once the companions of Buddhist monks. They arrived in Europe with the Dutch East India Company and became the favoured dogs of the House of Orange.

alertness, he gives the impression that he is leaning forward towards whatever his large lustrous eyes are gazing at.

He is a dog who tends to make people smile when they see him, because he is so convinced of his own importance. For such a stocky dog he can move fast. His slightly short nose sometimes causes him problems in hot weather as it restricts his breathing, but breeders tend to select for the wide nostrils, which will enable him to exercise as freely as he wishes.

◆ ABOVE
The stern expression of the Pug belies his real sense of fun.

BREED BOX	
Size	small
	25–28 cm
	(10–11 in), 6.3–8 kg
	(14–17½ lb)
Grooming	undemanding
Exercise	medium
Feeding	medium
Temperament	lively and cheerful

◆ RIGHT
The tightly curled tail balances the snub nose exactly, to produce a very tidy little dog

◆ ABOVE
The Pug is adaptable, sociable and good-natured and makes a good family dog.

YORKSHIRE TERRIER

The Yorkshire Terrier is a breed of two distinct types. The tiny dog, seen immaculately groomed in the show-ring, weighs up to 3.1 kg (7 lb). The jaunty dog seen on a lead in the street or racing joyfully around the park is the same dog, but often twice the size. The fact is that the long steel blue and bright tan hair that bedecks the glamour star of the shows would break off short if he ran loose. But the spirit of the true Yorkshire tyke is the same inside whatever the outward appearance.

◆ ABOVE
This Yorkie is groomed to perfection as befits a top dog.

Grooming the household companion, a dog that is immensely popular throughout the world, is easily accomplished with ordinary skills. As a home-loving animal, the Yorkie is tough, ready to play with the children or dispatch any rat unwise enough to invade his owner's dwelling.

◆ ABOVE
Companion Yorkies wear their coats shorter than these show dogs and do not require the same amount of artistry.

BREED BOX	
Size	very small maximum 3.1 kg (7 lb) dog: 20.5 cm (8 in) bitch: 18 cm (7 in)
Grooming	demanding
Exercise	medium
Feeding	undemanding
Temperament	alert and intelligent

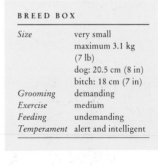

◆ RIGHT
This elegant display shows canine grooming at its most spectacular.

INDEX

Affenpinscher, 142
Afghan Hound, 8
Airedale Terrier, 58
Akita, Japanese, 86
Alaskan Malamute, 100
Alsatian *see* German Shepherd Dog
American Cocker Spaniel, 50
American Eskimo Dog, 114
American Foxhound, 21
Anatolian Shepherd Dog, 101
Australian Cattle Dog, 102
Australian Shepherd Dog, 102
Australian Silky Terrier, 143
Australian Terrier, 59

Basenji, 9
Basset Fauve de Bretagne, 10
Basset Hound, 11
Beagle, 13
Bearded Collie, 103
Bedlington Terrier, 59
Belgian Shepherd Dog, 104-5
Bergamasco, 105
Bernese Mountain Dog, 106
Bichon Frise, 144
Bloodhound, 14
Bolognese, 144
Border Collie, 107
Border Terrier, 60
Borzoi, 15
Boston Terrier, 80
Bouvier des Flandres, 108
Boxer, 109
Bracco Italiano, 34
Briard, 110
Brittany, 34

Brussels Griffon, 148
Buhund, Norwegian, 126
Bull Terrier, 61
Bulldog, 81
 French, 84
Bullmastiff, 111

Cairn Terrier, 62
Canaan Dog, 82
Cardigan Corgi (Welsh), 138
Cattle Dog, Australian, 102
Cavalier King Charles Spaniel, 145
Chesapeake Bay Retriever, 44
Chihuahua, 146
Chin, Japanese, 149
Chinese Crested Dog, 147
Chow Chow, 82
Clumber Spaniel, 49
Cocker Spaniel:
 American, 50
 English, 51
Collie,
 Bearded, 103
 Border, 107
 Rough, 112
 Smooth, 112
Corgi, Welsh 138-9
Curly Coated Retriever, 45
Czesky Terrier, 62

Dachshunds, 16-17
Dalmatian, 83
Dandie Dinmont, 63
Deerhound, 18
Dobermann, 113

Elkhound, 19
English Cocker Spaniel, 51
English Setter, 35
English Springer Spaniel, 52
 English Toy Terrier, 147
  Eskimo Dog, 114
  Estrela Mountain Dog, 115

  Finnish Lapphund, 116
  Finnish Spitz, 20
   Flat-coated Retriever, 46
   Fox Terrier:
    Smooth, 64
    Wire, 65
   Foxhound, 21
    American, 21
    French Bulldog, 84

German Shepherd Dog, 117
German Short-haired Pointer, 36
German Spitz, 85
German Wire-haired Pointer, 36
Glen of Imaal Terrier, 67
Golden Retriever, 47
Gordon Setter, 37
Grand Basset Griffon Vendeen, 10
Grand Bleu de Gascoigne, 21
Great Dane, 119
Greyhound, 22
 Italian, 149
Griffon Bruxellois, 148
Groenendael, 104
gundogs, 4, 33-55

Hamiltonstovare, 23
Harrier, 24
herding dogs *see* working dogs
hounds, 4, 7-31
Hovawart, 120
Hungarian Kuvasz, 120
Hungarian Puli, 121
Hungarian Vizsla, 38
Hungarian Wire-haired Vizsla, 38
Husky, Siberian, 135

Ibizan Hound, 25
Irish Red and White Setter, 39
Irish Setter, 40
Irish Terrier, 66
Irish Water Spaniel, 53
Irish Wolfhound, 26
Italian Greyhound, 149
Italian Hound, 25
Italian Spinone, 41

Jack Russell Terrier, 70
Japanese Akita, 86
Japanese Chin, 149
Japanese Shiba Inu, 86
Japanese Spitz, 87

Keeshond, 88
Kerry Blue Terrier, 67
King Charles Spaniel, 150
Komondor, 121
Kooikerhondje, 41
Kuvasz, Hungarian, 120

Labrador Retriever, 48
Laekenois, 104
Lakeland Terrier, 68

Lancashire Heeler, 122
Lapphund:
  Finnish, 116
  Swedish, 136
Large Munsterlander, 42
Leonberger, 89
Lhasa Apso, 90
Lowchen, 151

Malamute, Alaskan, 100
Malinois, 104-5
Maltese, 151
Manchester Terrier, 68
Maremma Sheepdog, 123
Mastiff, 124
  Bullmastiff, 111
  Neapolitan, 124
  Tibetan, 137
Miniature Pinscher, 152
Miniature Schnauzer, 91
Munsterlander, Large, 42

Neapolitan Mastiff, 124
Newfoundland, 125
Norfolk Terrier, 69
Norwegian Buhund, 126
Norwegian Lundehund, 27
Norwich Terrier, 69
Nova Scotia Duck-tolling Retriever, 42

Old English Mastiff, 124
Old English Sheepdog, 127
Otterhound, 28

Papillon, 153
Parson Jack Russell Terrier, 70
pedigree dogs, 4-5
Pekingese, 154
Pembroke Corgi, 139
Petit Basset Griffon
  Vendeen, 12
Pharaoh Hound, 27
Pinscher, 128
  Miniature, 152
Pointer, 43
  German Short-haired, 36
  German Wire-haired, 4, 36
Polish Lowland Sheepdog, 129
Pomeranian, 155
Poodles, 92-3
Portuguese Water Dog, 129
Pug, 156
Puli, Hungarian, 121

Pyrenean Mountain Dog, 130
Pyrenean Sheepdog, 130

Retrievers:
  Chesapeake Bay, 44
  Curly Coated, 45
  Flat-coated, 46
  Golden, 47
  Labrador, 48
  Nova Scotia Duck-tolling, 42
Rhodesian Ridgeback, 29
Rottweiler, 131
Rough Collie, 112

St Bernard, 132
Saluki, 30
Samoyed, 133
Schipperke, 94
Schnauzer, 94
  Giant, 118
  Miniature, 91
Scottish Terrier, 71
Sealyham Terrier, 72
Segugio Italiano, 25
Setter:
  English, 35
  Gordon, 37
  Irish, 40
  Irish Red and White, 39
Shar Pei, 95
Shetland Sheepdog, 134
Shiba Inu, Japanese, 86
Shih Tzu, 96
Siberian Husky, 135
Silky Terrier, Australian, 143
Skye Terrier, 73

Sloughi, 31
Smooth Collie, 112
Smooth Fox Terrier, 64
Soft-coated Wheaten Terrier, 74
Spaniel:
  American Cocker, 50
  Cavalier King Charles, 145
  Clumber, 49
  English Cocker, 51
  English Springer, 52
  Field, 52
  Irish Water, 53
  King Charles, 150
  Sussex, 54
  Tibetan, 97
  Welsh Springer, 54
Spinone, Italian, 41
Spitz:
  German, 85
  Japanese, 87
Springer Spaniel:
  English, 52
  Welsh, 54
Staffordshire Bull Terrier, 75
Sussex Spaniel, 54
Swedish Lapphund, 136
Swedish-Vallhund, 136

terriers, 5, 57-77
Tervueren, 104-5
Tibetan Mastiff, 137
Tibetan Spaniel, 97
Tibetan Terrier, 97
toy dogs, 5, 141-157

utility dogs, 5, 79-97

Vallhund, Swedish, 136
Vizsla, 38

Water Dog, Portuguese, 129
Water Spaniel, Irish, 53
Weimaraner, 55
Welsh Corgi, 138-9
Welsh Springer Spaniel, 54
Welsh Terrier, 76
West Highland White Terrier, 77
Whippet, 31
Wire Fox Terrier, 65
Wolfhound, Irish, 26
working dogs, 5, 99-139

Yorkshire Terrier, 157

ACKNOWLEDGEMENTS

The publishers would like to thank the following dog owners and breeders for their kind help with photography:

THE HOUND GROUP:
Afghan Hound: Mrs Pascoe; Basenji: S Woollard; Basset Hound: Mrs Pascoe; Basset Fauve de Bretagne: J Aldrich; Grand and Petit Basset Griffon Vendeen: Mrs Y Dean & Miss C Gutherless, R Phillips; Beagle: P Walden; Bloodhound: Mrs E Richards; Borzoi: Mr B O' Callaghan; Dachshunds: T Thomas, Mrs G E Taylor, J White, W Harris, M Endersby; Deerhound: S Finnett & H Heathcote; Elkhound: Mrs J Hibbert; Finnish Spitz: B K & B A Williams; Foxhound: J Goode; Grand Bleu de Gascoigne: E Bradic; Greyhound: J White; Hamiltonstovare: Mrs D Cooke; Harrier: Minehead Harriers; Ibizan Hound: A Wilde; Pharoah Hound: P Ayling; Irish Wolfhound: Miss A Bennett; Norwegian Lundehund: Mrs G E Sansom; Segugio Italiano: A Wilde; Otterhound: J Ashworth; Rhodesian Ridgeback: J Ellis; Saluki: Miss T Larkin; Sloughi: Miss S Harper & Mr R Read; Whippet: J White.

THE GUNDOG GROUP:
Bracco Italiano: Mr & Mrs J Shaw; Brittany: M. & Mrs M Beaven; English Setter: F Grimsdell; German Short-haired Pointer: P Robinson; German Wire-haired Pointer: Mr R Major; Gordon Setter: Mr P F Tye; Hungarian Vizsla: K Bicknell; Hungarian Wire-haired Vizsla: R Thompson; Irish Red and White Setter: Mrs P E Brigden; Irish Setter: M Gurney; Italian Spinone: C Fry; Koikerhondje: Mrs Whybrow; Large Munsterlander: Mrs Trowsdale; Nova Scotia Duck-tolling Retriever: Mr & Mrs D Hardings; Pointer: Mr & Mrs M Welsh; Chesapeake Bay Retriever: C Mayhew; Curly Coated Retriever: Mrs C Pilbeam; Flat Coated Retriever: L Irwin; Golden Retriever: C Fry; Labrador Retriever: C Coode; American Cocker Spaniel: Mrs Petty; Clumber Spaniel: Mrs Reynolds; English Cocker Spaniel: B Harris, S Oxford; English Springer Spaniel: Mr & Mrs D Miller; Field Spaniel: Mr & Mrs N R & J Park; Irish Water Spaniel: Mr M Ford; Sussex Spaniel: Mrs C M Mitchell; Welsh Springer Spaniel: J Luckett Roynon; Weimaraners: Mrs Shall, Mrs B Adlington.

THE TERRIER GROUP:
Airedale Terrier: Mary Swash; Australian Terrier: B & V Hodgson; Bedlington Terrier: Mr B Reeves; Border Terrier: L Aldrich; Bull Terrier: P Larkin; Cairn Terrier: D Winsley & K Holmes; Czesky Terrier: B Rice-Stringer; Dandie Dinmont: Mrs Draper-Andrews; Smooth Fox Terrier: Mrs Winstanley; Wire Fox Terrier: D Chads; Irish

Terrier: Mr K Anderson; Glen of Imaal Terrier: Mrs R Welch; Kerry Blue Terrier: Mr Watson; Lakeland Terrier: Mr & Mrs J Wright; Manchester Terrier: Mrs Eva; Norfolk Terrier: A Broughton; Norwich Terrier: D Jenkins; Parson Jack Russell: Mrs A Hughes; Scottish Terrier: Miss C Chapman; Sealyham Terrier: D Winsley & K Holmes; Skye Terrier: Mr & Mrs D Miller; Soft-coated Wheaten Terrier: Mrs Checketts; Staffordshire Bull Terrier: Alec Waters; Welsh Terrier: S Poole; West Highland White Terrier: Mr R Wilshaw.

THE UTILITY/NON-SPORTING GROUP:
Boston Terrier: Mr & Mrs Hounslow; Bulldog: Mr G Payne; Canaan Dog: Mr & Mrs E Minto; Chow Chow: Mrs M Bennett; Dalmatian: Miss C Hicks; French Bulldog: Mrs Stemp, Mrs Trigg; German Spitz: Mr, Mrs & Miss Bennett, S Edgson; Japanese Akita: J Feeney; Japanese Shiba Inu: M Atkinson & L Lane; Japanese Spitz: S Sparks; Keeshond: Mrs P Luckhurst; Leonberger: G Smith & J Feehan; Lhasa Apso: G Lock; Miniature Schnauzer: Mrs M R Bonnamy, Mrs T Jeffries; Poodles: Mrs A Corish, Mr & Mrs M Beaven, Mrs L Ellis; Schipperke: M Deats; Standard Schnauzer: Mrs Hatterell-Brown; Shar Pei: C Cavanagh; Shih Tzu: Mrs V Goodwin; Tibetan Spaniel: Mr & Mrs Minto; Tibetan Terrier: Mrs Draper-Andrews.

THE WORKING GROUP:
Alaskan Malamute: J Al-Haddad, A Allen; Anatolian Shepherd Dog: Anatolian Shepherd Dog Club of Great Britain; Australian Cattle Dog: Ms S Smyth; Australian Shepherd Dog: Mrs Fry; Bearded Collie: Mrs C Bennet; Belgian Shepherd Dogs: F Cosme & J Collis, Mr & Mrs M Ralph, S B Wyre & E Richardson, K M McIlherene; Bergamasco: S Band & C McCarthy; Bernese Mountain Dog: A Wells; Border Collie: F Cosme & J Collis; Bouvier des Flandres: C Pierpoint; Boxer: Mrs Cobb; Briard: E Pitt; Bullmastiff: Mrs J Gunn; Rough Collie: Mrs Burtenshaw; Smooth Collie: Misses S & M, & Mr L Clark; Dobermann: Mrs K Le Mare; Eskimo Dog: Mrs S Hull; Estrela Mountain Dog: Mrs E J Snowdon; Finnish Lapphund: Mrs T Jackson; German Shepherd Dog: Miss L Graham; Giant Schnauzer: T Jeffries, R Joy; Great Dane: Mrs K Le Mare; Hovawart: T Smith; Hungarian Kuvasz: T Koryniaka; Hungarian Puli: Mrs J Farnfield; Komondor: M P & E Froome; Lancashire Heeler: Mrs J Farnfield; Maremma Sheepdog: Mrs J Downes; Mastiff: Mr K Taylor; Neapolitan Mastiff: Ms V

Roach & Mr N Davis; Newfoundland: Messrs Cutts & Galvin; Norwegian Buhund: Mr M Guidhouse; Old English Sheepdog: L Powell; Pinscher: A Handly; Polish Lowland Sheepdog: Mr & Mrs C Hastie; Portuguese Water Dog: J Johns; Pyrenean Mountain Dog: Mr Duffell; Pyrenean Sheepdog: Mrs B Judson; Rottweiler: Mrs Boas; St Bernard: Mrs L Byles; Samoyed: J I Rees; Shetland Sheepdog: Mrs R Crossley; Siberian Husky: Mrs S Hull; Swedish Lapphund: Mrs Mackie; Swedish Vallhund: Mrs J Wilton; Tibetan Mastiff: K Childs; Welsh Corgi (Cardigan): Miss Tonkyn; Welsh Corgi (Pembroke): Miss S Taylor.

THE TOY GROUP:
Affenpinscher: Mrs A J Teasdale; Australian Silky Terrier: J Sharpe, Mr & Mrs B Faulkner & Mrs K Whiteford; Bichon Frise: C Wyatt; Bolognese: S & C McCarthy; Cavalier King Charles Spaniel: Mrs J Read; Chihuahua: Mrs K Le Mare; Chinese Crested Dog: R Tillman; English Toy Terrier: Mrs Bonifas; Griffon Bruxellois: Miss M Downey, Miss John; Italian Greyhound: Mrs M Sprague-White; Japanese Chin: M Moss; King Charles Spaniel: M Moss; Lowchen: J Creffield; Maltese: Mrs C Memsley; Miniature Pinscher: Mrs S Colborne Baber; Papillon: A Broughton; Pekingese: Misses A Summers & V Williams; Pomeranian: Mrs C McCutchon-Ciarke; Pug: Mr I Herold; Yorkshire Terrier: O A Sameja.

PHOTOGRAPHER'S ACKNOWLEDGEMENTS
I would like to express my thanks to the breeders and to: C Fry, L Graham, M Peacock, S Bradley, A Wells, P Beaven, J & P Canning, L & A Piatneuer, V Dyer, B Stnet and J Hay. Thanks also to Pampered Pets of Godalming, Colin Clarke Veterinary Practice, Çelia Cross Greyhound Rescue, Canine Partners for Indpendence and Weycolour Limited. Last but not least thanks to my partner Alison Hay for her administration and assistance.

NOTES

NOTES

NOTES

NOTES

NOTES

NOTES

NOTES

NOTES